Skills Practice
Workbook

Level 5
Book 2

McGraw Hill **SRA**

Columbus, OH

SRAonline.com

 **SRA**

Send all inquiries to this address:
SRA/McGraw-Hill
4400 Easton Commons
Columbus, OH 43219-6188

ISBN: 978-0-07-610483-3
MHID: 0-07-610483-4

1 2 3 4 5 6 7 8 9 QPD 13 12 11 10 09 08 07

The *McGraw·Hill* Companies

Unit 4 Our Corner of the Universe

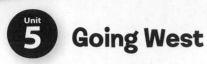

Unit 5 Going West

Unit 6 Call of Duty

Name _____ **Date** _____

Words with Greek Roots

Focus **Greek roots** are common in the English language. Identifying and understanding Greek roots can help you define difficult words. When you know the meaning of a root, you can figure out the meanings of many words that contain that root.

Practice Think of a word that uses each Greek root given below. Write the word on the line, and then use it in a sentence.

1. *tele* means "far away" _____

_____

_____

2. *tri* means "three"_____

_____

_____

3. *aqua* means "water" _____

_____

_____

4. *bio* means "life" _____

_____

_____

Apply Each group of words below uses the same Greek root. The roots' meanings are listed in the box. Use your knowledge of words to select the correct meaning, and write it on the line.

measure	eye	star	sound	study	water

5. phonograph, telephone, phonics, xylophone

   phon means _____

6. hydrant, dehydrated, hydroelectric

   hydro means _____

7. centimeter, speedometer, thermometer

   meter means _____

8. asteroid, astronomy, astronaut

   aster means _____

9. biology, psychology, geology, physiology

   ology means _____

10. optical, Cyclops, optician, optometrist

    ops means _____

Word Structure • *Skills Practice 2*

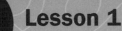
Name _____ Date _____

Selection Vocabulary

Focus

infinity (in•fin'•i•tē) *n.* the condition of having no limits (page 354)

disks (disks) *n.* plural of **disk:** a flat, thin, round object (page 356)

clusters (klus'•tərz) *n.* plural of **cluster:** a number of things of the same kind that are grouped together (page 357)

bulges (bəl'•jez) *n.* plural of **bulge:** a rounded part that swells out (page 357)

cosmic (koz'•mik) *adj.* of or relating to the universe (page 358)

spokes (spōks) *n.* plural of **spoke:** one of the rods or bars that connect the rim of a wheel to the hub (page 358)

galaxy (gal'•ək•sē) *n.* a very large group of stars (page 359)

spiral (spī'•rəl) *n.* a curve that keeps winding. A spiral may wind inward and outward or downward and upward (page 359)

collapse (kə•laps') *v.* to fall in; break down (page 360)

detect (di•tekt') *v.* to find out or notice; discover (page 360)

Practice **Circle the word that correctly completes each sentence.**

1. The spider crawled round and round in a _____ shape to spin its web.
   a. cosmic   **b.** spiral   **c.** bulges

2. Terrell's house of cards began to _____ when he sneezed.
   a. collapse   **b.** detect   **c.** spiral

3. _____ of diamonds hung from the princess's ears.
   a. bulges   **b.** spokes   **c.** clusters

4. I did not _____ any hints about the surprise party.
   a. spiral   **b.** detect   **c.** collapse

5. Numbers increase to _____ because they never end.
   a. galaxy   **b.** cosmic   **c.** infinity

6. A _____ may contain billions of stars.
   a. galaxy   **b.** spiral   **c.** cosmic

7. The _____ of the bicycle wheel were broken when he hit the curb.
   a. spokes   **b.** clusters   **c.** bulges

8. After long missions, scientists were unsure of the effects of _____ rays on astronauts.
   a. bulges   **b.** spiral   **c.** cosmic

9. The large _____ of the apparatus spinning.
   a. disks   **b.** infinity   **c.** detect

10. The _____ of the large balloon were almost ready to burst from all of the air.
    a. cosmic   **b.** bulges   **c.** spiral

Apply   Match each word to its definition on the right.

11. galaxy

12. clusters

13. collapse

14. disks

15. bulges

16. detect

a. rounded parts that swell out

b. to find out or notice

c. things of the same kind that are grouped together

d. to fall in, break down

e. a very large group of stars

f. flat, thin, round objects

Name _____ Date _____

Classify and Categorize

Focus
Classifying and categorizing are ways of organizing information. They can help you better understand and remember what you read.

- **Classifying** is identifying the similarities that objects, characters, or events have in common with each other, and then grouping them by their similarities.

- **Categorizing** is the act of organizing the objects, characters, or events into groups, or categories.

Practice
Look at the first page of "The Universe" and list five classifications found in the address.

1. _____

2. _____

3. _____

4. _____

5. _____

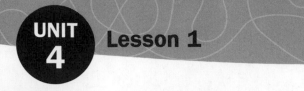

Apply On the diagram below, heavenly bodies are categorized as stars, planets, and constellations. Complete the diagram by thinking of things that could be classified under the headings *Stars, Planets,* or *Nebulas.*

Stars

Heavenly Bodies

Planets

Nebulas

Name _____ Date _____

Recording Concept Information

As I read the selection, this is what I added to my understanding of Our Corner of the Universe.

- "The Universe" by Seymour Simon

_____

_____

_____

- "Circles, Squares, and Daggers: How Native Americans Watched the Skies" by Elsa Marston

_____

_____

_____

- "The Mystery of Mars" by Sally Ride and Tam O'Shaugnessy

_____

_____

_____

- "Apollo 11: First Moon Landing" by Michael D. Cole

_____

_____

_____

- "Ellen Ochoa: Reaching for the Stars" by Claire Daniel

_____

_____

_____

Name _____ **Date** _____

Knowledge about Our Corner of the Universe

- This is what I know about our corner of the universe before reading the unit.

_____

_____

_____

_____

_____

_____

- These are some things about our corner of the universe that I would like to talk about and understand better.

_____

_____

_____

_____

_____

_____

Reminder: I should read this page again when I get to the end of the unit to see how much my ideas about our corner of the universe have changed.

Name _____ Date _____

Ideas about *Our Corner of the Universe*

Of the ideas discussed in class about *Our Corner of the Universe*, these are the ones I found most interesting.

_____

_____

_____

_____

_____

_____

_____

_____

_____

_____

_____

_____

_____

_____

_____

Ideas about *Our Corner of the Universe* (continued)

Write down the ideas you found most interesting about the selection "Circles, Squares, and Daggers: How Native Americans Watched the Skies." Dicuss your ideas with the class.

_____

_____

_____

_____

_____

_____

_____

_____

_____

_____

_____

_____

_____

_____

_____

_____

_____

_____

_____

Name _____ **Date** _____

Letter of Request

Think

Audience: Who will read your letter of request?

_____

Purpose: Why are you writing a letter of request?

_____

Prewriting

A letter of request is a type of business letter. Use the lines below to plan your request.

○
- Where will the letter be sent?_____

_____

_____

- What will your salutation be?_____

_____

- What information are you requesting and why? _____

_____

_____

○
- How do you want the reader to respond to your request?_____

_____

Now on a separate sheet of paper, put the information above into the form of a business letter.

Revising

Use this checklist to revise your letter of request.

☐ Did you put the date, your name, and your address in the top left corner?

☐ Is your request stated clearly in the first sentence?

☐ Did you explain why you want the information?

☐ Did you thank the reader for his or her help?

☐ Is your letter polite and businesslike?

Editing/Proofreading

Use this checklist to correct mistakes

☐ Did you follow the correct format for a business letter?

☐ Did you check for spelling errors?

☐ Did you capitalize the correct words?

☐ Did you indent the paragraphs? Remember that a business letter's paragraphs are not indented.

Publishing

Use this checklist to get your letter ready to mail.

☐ Write your letter on a clean sheet of paper, or type your letter on a computer and print it. Be sure to use the automatic business letter tool if you use a computer.

☐ Reread your letter for errors.

☐ Sign your letter.

☐ Address and proofread the envelope.

☐ Place the letter in the envelope.

☐ Put the correct postage on the envelope and mail it.

Name _____ **Date** _____

Spelling

Focus

- **Irregular plurals** do not follow the regular rules for forming plurals. They do not end in *-s* or *-es*. Sometimes the base word spelling changes to form the plural, and sometimes it does not change at all:
  child, children; salmon, salmon; person, people

- Understanding and identifying **Greek roots** and their meanings can help you define and spell difficult and unfamiliar words. Here are some of the Greek roots in the spelling words and their meanings:
  cycl = "circle" or "ring"; ***onym*** = "name"; ***astr*** and ***aster*** = "star"

Word List

1. asterisk
2. antonym
3. cycle
4. phenomena
5. alumnus
6. cyclone
7. radius
8. astronomy
9. index
10. phenomenon
11. bicycle
12. indices
13. alumni
14. synonym
15. stimulus
16. radii
17. disaster
18. asteroid
19. stimuli
20. astronaut

Practice **Each of the following examples includes at least one Greek root.**
Write the spelling word represented in each line.

1. bi + cycl + e = _____

2. aster + isk = _____

3. dis + aster = _____

4. cycl + one = _____

5. syn + onym = _____

6. aster + oid = _____

7. cycl + e = _____

8. astr + onomy = _____

9. ant + onym = _____

10. astr + onaut = _____

On the lines, write the singular and plural form of each spelling word beginning:

stimu-

11. singular: _____   16. plural: _____

12. plural: _____   **alum-**

phenome-   17. singular: _____

13. singular: _____   18. plural: _____

14. plural: _____   **rad-**

ind-   19. singular: _____

15. singular: _____   20. plural: _____

Apply If the underlined noun in the sentence is incorrect, write the correct form from the spelling list on the line. If it is correct, write *correct.*

21. Too many <u>stimuluses</u> make it hard to study.   _____

22. That book has two <u>indixes</u>.   _____

23. A thunderstorm is a natural <u>phenomena</u>.   _____

24. My father and mother are both <u>alumni</u> of Harding High   _____

25. A fiction book usually does not have an <u>indices</u>.   _____

26. The larger the circle, the longer its <u>radius</u>.   _____

27. Those two players are <u>phenomenas</u>!   _____

28. Her uncle is an <u>alumnu</u> of a state college.   _____

29. The pay raise was a <u>stimuli</u> for them to work harder.   _____

30. All <u>radii</u> in a circle are the same length.   _____

Name _____ Date _____

Demonstrative Pronouns and Hyphens

Focus

A **demonstrative pronoun** demonstrates by indicating or pointing out something. *This*, *these*, *that*, and *those* are demonstrative pronouns.

- To refer to things that are nearby, use *this,* singular, or *these,* plural.

- To refer to things that are far away, use *that,* singular, or *those,* plural.

- **This** is the shirt I will wear. Are **these** the papers you needed?

- **That** is the best idea so far. Where are you putting **those?**

Hyphens are used in the following cases:

- to divide a word between syllables when you run out of space on a line

- for some compound nouns
  good-bye   *teeter-totter*   *sister-in-law*

- when forming a compound modifier, such as an adjective formed from two words written in front of a noun
  second-place finish   *orange-red sun*   *Chicago-style pizza*

- for numbers and fractions that are written out
  ninety-nine   *forty-six*   *one-fourth*

Practice

Use the clue in parentheses to choose a demonstrative pronoun that will correctly complete each sentence. Also, place hyphens where they are missing.

1. _____ was Samantha's last chance to reach first place. (far away)

2. _____ recipe uses one fourth cup of sugar. (nearby)

3. How will Uncle Reuben know if _____ pizza slices are Chicago style? (far away)

4. Give me a hand with _____ ice cubes before they all melt. (nearby)

Apply *This, these, that,* and *those* are not always pronouns. They are adjectives when they modify nouns, as in *this house* or *those people.* In each sentence, determine whether *this, these, that,* or *those* is used as a pronoun or an adjective. Write *P* for pronoun or *A* for adjective. Also, place hyphens where they are missing.

5. Do you remember Nagid, **that** boy who moved to

   Dallas Fort Worth last year? _____

6. We do not know who put **this** here, but it needs to move

   one-half inch to the left. _____

7. I pulled **these** closer so I could reach them with my

   salad-fork. _____

8. What are **those** things on Brijesh's swing-set?

   _____

9. Could you tell her **that** shirt isn't blue green?

   _____

10. I need help with **those** twenty two math questions.

    _____

11. Would you give **this** to my brother in law?

    _____

12. Rubber bands should hold **these** together.

    _____

Name _____ Date _____

Multiple-Meaning Words and Suffix *-tion/-ion*

Multiple-meaning words are words that have more than one meaning, but the same origin. You will often need to look at context clues to figure out which meaning is being used in a particular sentence.

The suffix *-tion/-ion* is used to turn words into nouns.

Compose (verb) + *-tion* = composition

Propose (verb) + *-tion* = proposition

Add the suffix to the following words. Write the word on the line and provide at least two meanings for the resulting multiple-meaning word.

1. apply

_____

_____

2. reserve

_____

_____

3. inflate

_____

_____

Apply | Add the suffix *-tion/-ion* to each word below to create a multiple-meaning word. On the lines provided, use the resulting word in two sentences. Each sentence should reflect a different meaning.

4. project _____

_____

_____

_____

5. form _____

_____

_____

_____

6. direct _____

_____

_____

_____

7. deposit _____

_____

_____

_____

8. operate _____

_____

_____

_____

Name _____ Date _____

Selection Vocabulary

Focus

stargazers (stär'•gā•zerz) *n.* plural of **stargazer:** a person who studies the stars (page 370)

observatories (əb•zûr•və•tor•ēz) *n.* plural of **observatory:** a place designed for astronomers to study the stars (page 370)

archaeology (är'•kē•ol'•ə•jē) *n.* Archaeologists dig up the remains of ancient cities and towns and then study the tools, weapons, pottery, and other things they find. (page 370)

abandoned (ə•ban'•dənd) *v.* past tense of **abandon:** to leave and not return (page 370)

devised (di•vīzd') *v.* past tense of **devise:** to think out, invent, or plan (page 370)

dramatic (drə•ma'•tik) *adj.* exciting or interesting (page 371)

calculations (kal'•kyə•lā'•shənz) *n.* plural of **calculation:** the result of counting, computing, or figuring (page 373)

vertical (vûr'•ti•kəl) *adj.* straight up and down (page 375)

bull's-eye (boolz•ī') *n.* the center of a circle or target (page 377)

solar (sō'•lər) *adj.* having to do with or coming from the sun (page 378)

Practice Write *T* in the blank if the sentence for the vocabulary word is correct. Write *F* if the sentence is false. For every *F* answer, write the vocabulary word that fits the definition.

1. *Stargazers* are places to study the stars. ____ _____

2. The center of a circle or target is a *bull's-eye*. ____ _____

3. Something *vertical* is exciting or interesting. ____ _____

4. *Calculations* are the result of counting, computing, or figuring.

   ____ _____

5. A project that has been *devised* has been thought out, invented, or planned. ____ _____

6. *Solar* means "coming from the sun."

   ____ _____

7. A person who *abandoned* his or her home left and did not return.

   ____ _____

8. *Archaeology* is the study of the life and culture of people

   of the past. ____ _____

9. *Observatories* are people who study the stars.

   ____ _____

 Apply **Review the vocabulary words and definitions from** ***Circles, Squares, and Daggers: How Native Americans*** ***Watched the Skies.* Write two sentences that each use at least one of the vocabulary words from this lesson.**

10. _____

    _____

11. _____

    _____

Name _____ Date _____

Compare and Contrast

Focus Writers compare and contrast to paint a clearer picture of the people and things they are writing about.

- To **compare** means to tell how things, ideas, events, or characters are alike.

- To **contrast** means to tell how things, ideas, events, or characters are different.

 **Practice** The author of "Circles, Squares, and Daggers" describes how ancient Native Americans observed the sky. On the lines below, compare and contrast two things each about the Bighorn Medicine Wheel observatory and the observatories used by the Anasazi.

Compare

1. _____

_____

_____

_____

Contrast

2. _____

_____

_____

_____

Apply

Read each sentence and tell whether it shows a comparison or a contrast. Then, rewrite each sentence to reflect the other term, either compare or contrast. Note the change that occurs in the meaning.

3. Dave and Ed both finished all their vegetables. _____

_____

4. Martha plays the trombone, while Janet plays the cello. _____

_____

5. I like to read mysteries just like my sister Gina. _____

_____

6. Both cats and dogs make good pets. _____

_____

7. Jacob and Jason are twins, but Jacob is slightly taller. _____

_____

Name _____ **Date** _____

Formulating Questions and Problems

A good question or problem to investigate:

_____

_____

_____

_____

Why this is an interesting question or problem:

_____

_____

_____

_____

Some other things I wonder about this question
or problem:

_____

_____

_____

_____

Formulating Questions and Problems (continued)

My investigation group's question or problem:

_____

_____

_____

_____

What our investigation will contribute to the rest
of the class:

_____

_____

_____

_____

Some other things I wonder about this question
or problem:

_____

_____

_____

_____

Inquiry • *Skills Practice 2*

Name _____ Date _____

Book Review

Think — **Audience: Who** will read your book review?

_____

Purpose: What do you want your book review to do?

_____

Prewriting — Use the organizer below to plan your book review.

○ Title: _____

Author's Purpose: _____

Summary: _____

_____

_____

_____

Your Opinions: _____

○ _____

_____

Your Recommendation: _____

_____

Revising

Use this checklist to revise your book review.

☐ Did you use formal language in your writing?

☐ Did you use a thesaurus to choose precise and vivid words?

☐ Are your opinions explained with examples?

☐ Will your ideas convince others to read or not read the story?

Editing/Proofreading

Use this checklist to correct mistakes

☐ Did you spell the title and author's name correctly?

☐ Did you check all capitalization and punctuation including hyphens?

☐ Did you check your spelling of possessive nouns?

☐ Have you correctly used demonstrative pronouns?

Publishing

Use this checklist to prepare for publication.

☐ Write neatly or type on a computer to create a final copy. Be sure to use the correct formatting.

☐ Provide illustrations for your review or a photograph of the author.

Name _____   Date _____

Spelling

Focus

Nouns are formed when the suffix **-tion/-ion** is added to a base or root word. If a word already ends in *t,* then simply add *-ion*. If a word ends in *e,* drop the *e* before adding the ending. Finally, in some cases, the base word changes in spelling before the *-tion/-ion* ending is added, as in *attend, attention*.

Practice

On the lines, write the spelling words that are formed from the following base words and suffixes.

1. pollute + ion = _____

2. suggest + ion = _____

3. abolish + tion = _____

4. obstruct + ion = _____

5. construct + ion = _____

6. subtract + ion = _____

7. reflect + ion = _____

8. retain + tion = _____

9. deflect + ion = _____

10. revolve + tion = _____

11. intersect + ion = _____

12. attend + tion = _____

13. re + tribute + ion = _____

14. institute + ion = _____

Word List

1. construction
2. subtraction
3. intersection
4. attention
5. institution
6. retribution
7. obstruction
8. contradiction
9. retraction
10. abolition
11. suggestions
12. instruction
13. contribution
14. revolution
15. selection
16. detection
17. pollution
18. reflection
19. retention
20. deflection

15. contradict + ion = _____

16. instruct + ion = _____

17. retract + ion = _____

18. contribute + ion = _____

19. select + ion = _____

20. detect + ion = _____

Apply

On the line, write the spelling word that is related by a common root or base word to each of the following words.

21. pollute _____

22. retracted _____

23. suggested _____

24. contradicted _____

25. attentive _____

26. subtracted _____

27. instructed _____

28. detectable _____

29. intersected _____

30. contributed _____

Fill in the missing letters and write the resulting spelling words correctly on the lines below.

31. construc_____n _____

32. revo_____n _____

33. obstruc_____n _____

34. sele_____n _____

35. refle_____n _____

36. rete_____n _____

37. defl_____n _____

38. abol_____n _____

39. instit_____n _____

40. retri_____n _____

Name _____ **Date** _____

Formatting

Formatting is how text is organized and presented on a printed page. The format can change depending on what you write and who your audience is. For example, a letter of request would not be formatted in the same way as a research report would be.

Choose the formatting term for a business letter that best fits in the sentences.

heading	inside address	salutation
body	closing	signature

1. The _____ goes two lines below the body at the left margin.

2. Your _____ goes under the closing.

3. The _____ consists of the sender's address and the date. It goes in the upper left corner.

4. The _____ is the greeting. A colon always goes after it.

5. The _____ includes the name and address of the person receiving the letter. It goes two lines below the heading.

6. The _____ is the main part of the letter. It contains what you want to say. It begins two lines below the salutation, and is single-spaced.

Apply   Circle the letter of the answer that correctly completes each sentence about formatting an academic paper. You might want to have a word-processing program open during this exercise.

7. To add a header to your paper, you must first
   a. click View. **b.** open a new file. **c.** save your work.

8. The title of your paper should always be
   a. underlined. **b.** boldfaced. **c.** centered.

9. The empty spaces on the top, bottom, and sides of a paper are called
   a. tabs. **b.** headers **c.** margins.

10. The font size tells you how big the
    a. spaces between lines will be. **b.** letters will be. **c.** page will be.

11. An academic paper should be
    a. single-spaced. **b.** double-spaced. **c.** triple-spaced.

12. To properly indent each paragraph, use
    a. the backspace key. **b.** the spacebar. **c.** the tab key.

13. To change the line spacing on text you have already written, you must first
    a. click Tools. **b.** close the file. **c.** highlight the text.

Name _____ Date _____

Word Origins, Prefix *inter-*, and Suffix *-sion*

Focus Recognizing and understanding word origins can help you understand new and unfamiliar words. For example, the word *microscopic* appears in "The Mystery of Mars." It contains the Greek root *scop.* This root means "to look at." The prefix *micro-* means "very small." Thus *microscopic* literally means "too small to be seen."

The suffix *-sion* is used to change words into nouns.

> Comprehend + *-sion* = comprehension

> Propose + *-sion* = proposition

The prefix *inter-* means "between, among" or "through, across" when added to a base word.

> *Inter-* + planetary = interplanetary (across the distance between the planets)

> *Inter-* + session = intersession (between academic periods)

Practice Write the definition of the word made from combining the root words and affixes provided.

1. Prefix *inter-*
Latin root: *rupt* meaning to break

Interrupt means _____

2. Prefix *inter-*
Latin root: *lude* meaning to play

Interlude means _____

3. Suffix *-sion*
Latin root: *div* meaning to separate

Division means _____

Apply Write the word with the suffix *–sion* or the prefix *inter-* that best fits the definition. Then use each word in a sentence. Identify the base word and look up each word in the dictionary and provide the origin of each base or root word.

international interstate	decision discussion	intergalactic intercept	confusion confession

4. Open debate of a question or topic _____

_____

_____

5. Going through several states _____

_____

_____

6. Between or through galaxies _____

_____

_____

7. Act or result of making up one's mind _____

_____

_____

8. Across or among several nations _____

_____

_____

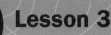

Name _____ Date _____

Selection Vocabulary

Focus

impact (im'•pakt') *n.* the force of one object striking against another (page 388)

deflated (di•flāt'•əd) *v.* past tense of **deflate:** to let the air out of something (page 388)

analyze (an'•ə•līz') *v.* to find out what something is made of by taking it apart (page 390)

texture (teks'•chür) *n.* the look and feel of something (page 390)

hospitable (hos•pi'•ti•bəl) *adj.* welcome and comfortable; friendly (page 390)

microscopic (mī•krō•skop'•ik) *adj.* something so small it can be seen only through a microscope (page 390)

harsh (härsh') *adj.* very severe (page 391)

haze (hāz) *n.* mist, smoke, or dust in the air (page 392)

accumulate (ə'•kyūm'•yə•lāt') *v.* to gather or pile up (page 393)

pressure (pre'•shər) *n.* force caused by one thing pushing against another thing (page 394)

Practice Write the word that best fits each clue below.

1. I drove over a nail, and my tire went flat. What did the nail

do to the tire? _____

2. My aunt invited me to her home and fed me a delicious home-cooked

meal. Which word describes my aunt? _____

3. This word describes the rough feel of sandpaper. Which word is it? _____

4. The desert air was extremely hot and the heat was severe. Which word describes the desert weather? _____

5. This word can describe germs, cells, and bacteria. Which word is it? _____

6. Morgan and Mariah pushed on the jammed door to try to open it. What were they using? _____

7. The dirty clothes are starting to pile up in the laundry room. Which word describes this? _____

8. Scientists do this to accumulated data. What do they do? _____

9. The morning fog casts this over everything. What does it cast? _____

10. The force of the asteroid colliding with Earth left a crater. Which word describes the force? _____

Apply

Write the word that best matches the underlined word or phrase in the sentences below.

11. The weather this winter has been <u>very severe</u>. _____

12. The <u>look and feel</u> of sandpaper is rough. _____

13. The algae were <u>too small for us to see</u>. _____

14. Blair <u>let the air out of</u> the balloon. _____

15. The <u>force</u> of the wrecking ball caused the building to collapse. _____

16. The <u>mist, smoke, or dust in the air</u> made my eyes water. _____

Name _____ **Date** _____

Making Conjectures

Our question or problem:

_____

_____

_____

_____

_____

_____

Conjecture (my first theory or explanation):

_____

_____

_____

_____

_____

As you collect information, your conjecture will change. Return to this page to record your new theories or explanations about your question or problem.

Our Corner of the Universe

My group's question or problem:

_____

_____

_____

_____

Knowledge Needs—Information I need to find or figure out in order to investigate the question or problem:

A. _____

B. _____

C. _____

D. _____

E. _____

Source	Useful?	How?
Encyclopedias		
Books		
Magazines		
Newspapers		
Video and Audio Clips		
Television		
Interviews, observations		
Museums		
Other:		

Name _____ Date _____

Science Fiction Story

Audience: Who will read your science fiction story?

_____

Purpose: What do you want your readers to think about your story?

_____

Prewriting Use this graphic organizer to plan your story.

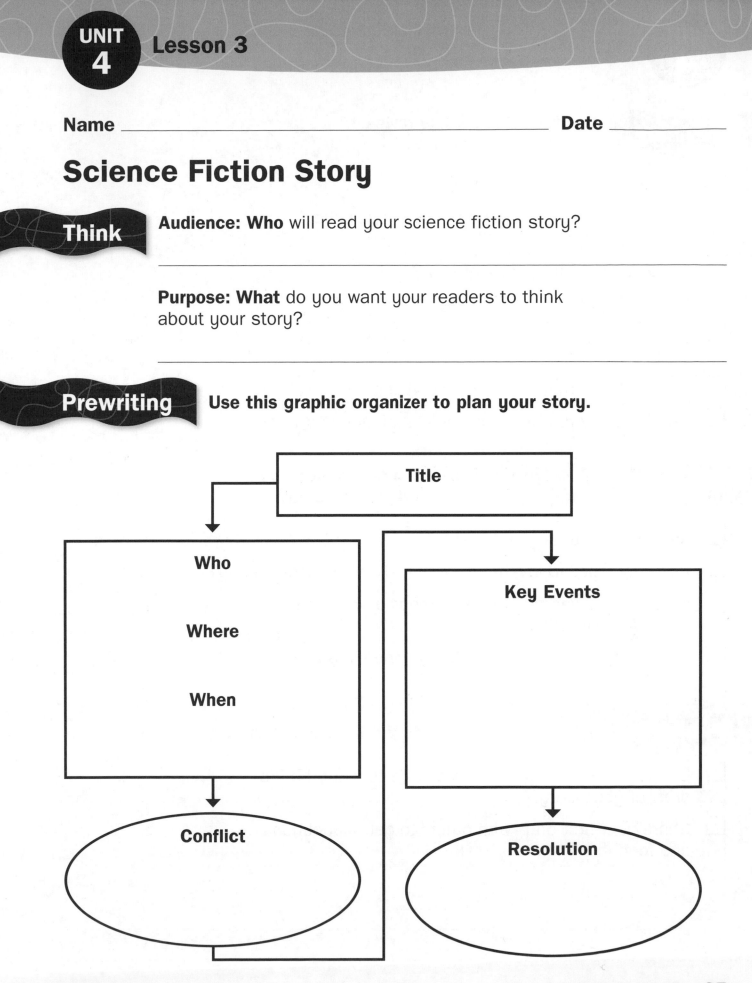

Revising

Use this checklist to revise your graphic organizer.

☐ Is your story set in the future?

☐ Does your story include some kind of science or technology?

☐ Have you chosen a point of view?

☐ Does your story have a conflict or problem?

☐ Have you decided how the characters will resolve the conflict?

☐ Does your story have rising action and a climax?

☐ Does your story have a beginning, middle, and end?

Editing/Proofreading

Use this checklist to edit your graphic organizer.

☐ Are proper nouns capitalized?

☐ Have you spelled invented words and names consistently?

☐ If you have invented names for people or places, are the names believable?

☐ Do the key events of your story happen in a logical order?

Publishing

Use this checklist to write your first draft.

☐ Use the graphic organizer as a guide to write the first draft of your story.

☐ Share your first draft with others to get suggestions and feedback.

Name _____ Date _____

Spelling

- A prefix changes the meaning of the base word it precedes. Identifying prefixes and understanding their meanings can help you figure out the meaning and spelling of a difficult or unfamiliar word. The prefix **inter-** means "among" or "between." For example, *interstate* means "between states."

- The suffix **-ly** changes an adjective to an adverb—*sad* to *sadly,* for example. The spelling of the base word does not change, unless it ends in *y.* In this case, change the *y* to *i* and add the *-ly.*

- The suffix **-sion** is like the suffixes *-tion/-ion.* It means "the state or quality of," and is added to verbs to make them nouns, as in *decision.* The suffix *-sion* is often added to verbs that end in a long vowel plus *de—decide, decision.* Drop the *-de* and add the *-sion* ending.

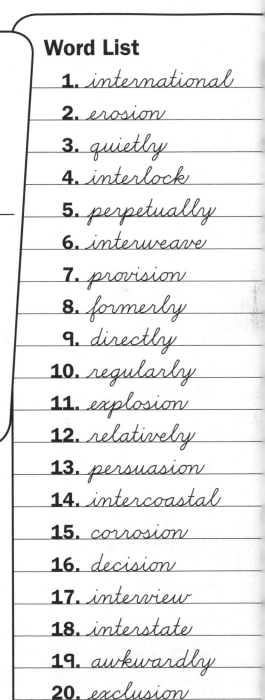

Word List

1. international
2. erosion
3. quietly
4. interlock
5. perpetually
6. interweave
7. provision
8. formerly
9. directly
10. regularly
11. explosion
12. relatively
13. persuasion
14. intercoastal
15. corrosion
16. decision
17. interview
18. interstate
19. awkwardly
20. exclusion

Practice Add the prefix *inter-* to the following base words to form spelling words from the list. Write the words on the line.

1. inter + state = _____

2. inter + view = _____

3. inter + weave = _____

4. inter + national = _____

5. inter + lock = _____

6. inter + coastal = _____

Add the suffixes *-ly* or *-sion* to the following base words to form spelling words from the list, and write them on the lines.

7. erode – de + sion =

8. regular + ly =

9. decide – de + sion =

10. persuade – de + sion =

11. quiet + ly =

12. provide – de + sion =

13. direct + ly =

14. relative + ly =

15. corrode – de + sion =

16. former + ly =

17. exclude – de + sion =

18. explode – de + sion =

19. awkward + ly =

20. perpetual + ly =

Apply

On the line, write the spelling word that is related by a common root or base word to each of the following words.

21. eroded

22. locking

23. weaving

24. irregular

25. perpetual

26. persuasive

27. undecided

28. coastline

29. former

30. explosive

31. relation

32. state

33. indirect

34. nation

35. provide

36. preview

37. corroded

38. excluded

39. awkwardness

40. quietness

Name _____ Date _____

Independent and Dependent Clauses

A **clause** is a group of words that has a subject and a verb.

Rule	Example
• An **independent clause** can stand alone as a sentence.	• I found the book in the fiction section.
• A **dependent clause** has a subject and a verb, but it cannot stand alone as a sentence.	• I found the book **that Julie needed for school** in the fiction section.
• **Dependent clauses** modify words in sentences. They are used as either adjectives or adverbs.	• *That Julie needed for school* modifies the noun *book*, so it is being used as an adjective.

Practice Label each example below with *I* for an independent clause or *D* for a dependent clause.

1. _____ That dog always makes me nervous.

2. _____ Because Mr. Gupta usually rides the subway.

3. _____ After the rain began pouring down.

4. _____ Aaron likes to go biking.

5. _____ That Paul wanted to purchase.

The following sentences contain independent and dependent clauses. Circle each dependent clause and underline each independent clause. Remember to look for relative pronouns and subordinating conjunctions as clues.

6. Thanh will go to the state finals if he wins the next match.

7. The volcano, which people thought was dormant, began rumbling loudly.

8. Unless you study, you might not pass the test.

9. After school, Marika walks to the bakery where her mother works.

10. The astronauts traveled where no other humans had gone before.

11. Because there were so many mosquitoes, we moved our picnic inside.

12. The man whose truck blocked our driveway apologized to my mom.

13. Clio was not allowed to go to the movies until she cleaned her room.

14. The place that Devon visited most often was the library.

15. The planet Mars is where I would like to live someday.

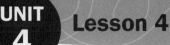

Name _____ Date _____

Synonyms and Antonyms

Antonyms are words with opposite, or nearly opposite, meanings. An antonym for *empty* is *full,* and an antonym for *dull* is *exciting.*

Synonyms are words with the same, or nearly the same, meaning. A synonym for *empty* is *vacant,* and a synonym for *dull* is *boring.*

Each word below is followed by two words. Circle the *antonym.*

1.	extraordinary	rare	normal
2.	anchored	moving	fixed
3.	left	joined	departed
4.	captured	trapped	released
5.	drop	fall	climb
6.	loud	silent	noisy

Each word below is followed by two words. Circle the synonym.

7.	lost	misplaced	found
8.	built	destroyed	constructed
9.	remote	nearby	distant
10.	tense	stressed	relaxed
11.	carefully	cautiously	recklessly
12.	completely	partly	entirely

Apply

Write a new sentence using an antonym for the underlined word in each sentence below. Underline the antonym you used in your sentence.

13. Nitesh's <u>usual</u> lunch consisted of a sandwich and a piece of fruit.

_____

_____

14. The attorney visited the office to discuss a <u>serious</u> legal issue.

_____

_____

Write a new sentence using a synonym for the underlined word in each sentence below. Underline the synonym you used in your sentence.

15. It is important to stay <u>focused</u> when you are taking a test.

_____

_____

16. The car's <u>exterior</u> was dented and scratched, but the engine worked fine.

_____

_____

Name _____ Date _____

Selection Vocabulary

Focus

module (mä'•jəl) *n.* a part of a spacecraft that has a special use and can be separated from the rest of the craft (page 406)

bulky (bəl'•kē) *adj.* large and puffy (page 406)

focused (fō•kəst) *v.* past tense of **focus:** to direct attention to someone or something (page 408)

thrust (thrust) *n.* a sudden, strong push or force (page 410)

hatch (hach) *n.* an opening in the deck of a ship or spacecraft that leads to other decks (page 413)

tranquility (tran•kwil'•ə•tē) *n.* the absence of motion or disturbance (page 414)

awe (ô) *n.* great wonder, fear, and respect (page 421)

depressed (di•prest') *v.* past tense of **depress:** to be sunk below the surrounding region (page 420)

mankind (man'•kīnd) *n.* human beings as a group; the human race (page 422)

sensations (sen•sā'•shənz) *n.* plural of **sensation:** feeling (page 422)

Practice   Write the word from the word box that matches each definition below.

sensations	module	awe	depressed
thrust	bulky	focused	tranquility
	mankind	hatch	

1. _____ great wonder, fear, and respect

2. _____ sunk below the surrounding area

3. _____ large and puffy

4. _____ human beings as a group

5. _____ a sudden, strong push or force

6. _____ the absence of motion or disturbance

7. _____ directed attention to someone or something

8. _____ a part of a spacecraft that has a special use and can be separated from the rest of the craft

9. _____ feelings

10. _____ an opening in the deck of a ship or spacecraft that leads to other decks

Apply Write the vocabulary word that best matches the underlined word or phrase in the sentences below.

11. When Julia caught a glimpse of the Grand Canyon, she was

   filled with <u>wonder and amazement</u> _____

12. I had many happy <u>feelings</u> when my younger sister was born.

   _____

13. Audrey climbed through the <u>opening in the deck of a spacecraft</u>

   and prepared for her spacewalk. _____

14. We could feel the <u>sudden, strong force</u> when the roller coaster

   took off. _____

Name _____ Date _____

Drawing Conclusions

Focus Writers cannot describe every detail about people or events in a story. Good readers draw conclusions using the information they have been given. **Drawing conclusions** means using the information in the text to make a statement about a person or event. The conclusion is not stated by the author, but the information in the text supports it.

Practice Reread pages 416–417 of "Apollo 11: First Moon Landing." What conclusion can you draw about Neil Armstrong based on the text? Write your conclusion below, and then support it with information from the text.

Conclusion:

_____

Information that supports my conclusion:

1. _____

_____

_____

2. _____

_____

_____

Apply Think of someone you admire, and then write a paragraph below showing why you look up to this person. Do not say how you feel. Instead, provide information that leads a reader to conclude that your subject is someone you admire.

_____

_____

_____

_____

_____

_____

_____

_____

_____

_____

_____

_____

_____

_____

_____

_____

_____

Comprehension Skill • _Skills Practice 2_

Name _____ **Date** _____

Science Fiction Story

Think

Audience: Who will read your science fiction story?

_____

Purpose: What do you want your readers to think about your story?

_____

Prewriting Once you have written the first draft of your story, share it with others to get their feedback. You can decide whether or not to use their ideas, but listen carefully to each one. Someone may have the perfect solution to a problem you are having with your story. On the lines below, write three ideas you were given to improve your story. Then decide how you will use each one.

1. Suggestion: _____

_____

Decision: _____

2. Suggestion: _____

_____

Decision: _____

3. Suggestion: _____

_____

Decision: _____

Revising
Use this checklist to revise your story.

- ☐ Is the point of view consistent throughout your story?
- ☐ Does your opening sentence grab the reader's attention?
- ☐ Have you created vivid characters with your descriptions?
- ☐ Do the events of your plot occur in a logical sequence?
- ☐ Does the tension rise as your story moves toward the climax? Have you added foreshadowing?

Editing/Proofreading
Use this checklist to correct mistakes.

- ☐ Did you use a thesaurus to find precise and descriptive words?
- ☐ Did the spelling of invented words remain the same throughout your story?
- ☐ Have you corrected run-on sentences and fragments?
- ☐ Did you correctly place quotation marks in your dialogue?
- ☐ Did you correctly use commas to separate clauses in complex sentences?

Publishing
Use this checklist to prepare your story for publication.

- ☐ Rewrite your story neatly in your best cursive handwriting.
- ☐ Illustrate your story with drawings, clip art, or other graphics.

Name _____ **Date** _____

Spelling

- **Synonyms** are words with the same, or nearly the same, meaning. For example, *cold* and *chilly* are synonyms.

- **Antonyms** are words with opposite, or nearly opposite, meanings. For example, *cheap* and *expensive* are antonyms.

You can find synonyms and antonyms for words in a thesaurus. Use synonyms and antonyms to help you remember the meaning of a new word.

Practice On the lines, write the groups of words from the word list that are synonyms. Use a thesaurus or dictionary if necessary.

1. _____

2. _____

3. _____

4. _____

5. _____

6. _____

7. _____

8. _____

9. _____

10. _____

Word List

1. graceful
2. prohibit
3. exceed
4. opposition
5. fatigue
6. distant
7. forbid
8. restrict
9. secluded
10. surpass
11. commencement
12. similarity
13. energy
14. outlandish
15. difference
16. conclusion
17. alliance
18. strange
19. clumsy
20. remote

On the lines, write the pairs of words from the word list that are antonyms.
Use a thesaurus or dictionary if necessary.

11. _____   15. _____   19. _____

12. _____   16. _____   20. _____

13. _____   17. _____

14. _____   18. _____

Apply   For each word below, list the spelling words that are synonyms on the lines. Use a thesaurus or dictionary if necessary.

isolated

1. _____

2. _____

3. _____

weird

4. _____

5. _____

ban

6. _____

7. _____

8. _____

outdo

9. _____

10. _____

For each word below, write the spelling word that is a synonym in the synonym column. Then write the spelling word that is an antonym in the antonym column. Use a thesaurus or dictionary if necessary.

	Synonym	Antonym
11. beginning	_____	_____
12. liveliness	_____	_____
13. likeness	_____	_____
14. partnership	_____	_____
15. awkward	_____	_____

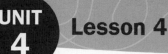

Name _____ Date _____

Apostrophes and Quotation Marks

Focus

Apostrophes are used to show possession and to form contractions.

- For most singular nouns, add 's.
- cat's ears, boss's necktie

- For plural nouns that end with s, add an apostrophe.
- flowers' petals troops' uniforms

- For singular proper nouns that end in s, add 's.
- the Harris's backyard Chris's haircut

A **contraction** is formed by combining two words and omitting one or more letters. An apostrophe replaces the missing letters.

do not, don't   we will, we'll   you have, you've

- **Quotation marks** are used to enclose a direct quotation. Periods and commas go inside the quotation marks.

- Place the exclamation point or question mark inside the quotation marks when it is part of the quotation, and outside when it is part of the entire sentence.

Example The librarian asked, "Please be quiet."

Practice Add quotation marks to the following sentences where needed.

1. What kind of vegetables dont you like? asked Mom.

2. Didnt Mom say, Watch your brother?

3. The announcer said, The games officially over.

4. Gary shouted, Stay with Louis dog!

5. Hard works the key to success, Dads boss always says.

Apply The apostrophes and quotation marks in the following sentences are missing or used incorrectly. Rewrite each sentence correctly.

6. King George did'nt need anyones help reading John Hancocks' giant signature.

_____

_____

7. Our teacher said Because of Americas constitution, "wer'e guaranteed certain rights that ca'nt be taken away."

_____

_____

8. Would youve been for the "Rebel's or the Tories'" during the Revolution? Rufus asked.

_____

_____

9. Riding hi"s horse as fast as he could Paul Revere shouted 'The British are coming!'.

_____

_____

10. Thomas Paines writings weren"t very popular in "England", said Mr. Stevens.

_____

_____

Name _____ Date _____

Homographs and the Prefix *photo-*

Focus

Homographs are words that are spelled the same but have different meanings and different origins. Sometimes homographs have different pronunciations because the stress is placed on a different syllable.

The prefix **photo-** is from Greek meaning "light." Read the literal meaning of the following word with the prefix *photo-:*

> *Photo-* + meter = to measure light

Practice

Write the word with the prefix *photo-* that matches each definition below.

photocopy	photosynthesis	photometer

1. Copy of printed material made through the action of light

_____

2. Synthesizing food for plants with the aid of light _____

3. Instrument used for measuring the intensity of light _____

Identify the base word used above that is a homograph and write two of the word's meanings.

_____

_____

_____

Apply Circle the homographs in the sentences below. Remember that some homographs have different pronunciations. Write the definition of the word as used in the sentence on the line. Using the word with the prefix *photo-* listed, write another sentence using one of the homograph's alternate meanings.

4. The president will address the people on television.

photograph _____

_____

_____

5. We were content to lie on the beach all day.

photosynthesis _____

_____

_____

6. The desert is a dry place with miles of sand.

photoelectric _____

_____

_____

7. He would set the tape player to record his favorite radio program.

photocopy _____

_____

_____

8. The woman used a file to smooth the customer's fingernails.

photogenic _____

_____

_____

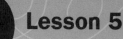
Name _____ Date _____

Selection Vocabulary

Focus

transferring (trəns•fûr'•ing) *v.* moving from one place to another (page 434)

responsibilities (ri•spon'•sə•bil'•i•tēz) *n.* plural of **responsibility:** something that is a person's job, duty, or concern (page 434)

confidence (kon'•fi•dəns) *n.* faith in oneself (page 434)

discouraged (di•skûr'•ijd') *v.* past tense of **discourage:** to try to keep a person from doing something (page 437)

application (ap'•li'•kā•shən) *n.* a request, especially for a job (page 437)

processes (pros'•es'•iz) *n.* plural of **process:** a series of actions performed in making or doing something (page 438)

eclipse (i•klips') *n.* a darkening or hiding of the sun, a planet, or a moon, by another heavenly body (page 441)

precise (prē•sīs') *adj.* exact; definite (page 442)

varies (vâr'•ēz) *v.* changes; makes or becomes different (page 442)

advance (ad•vans') *v.* to help the progress or growth of; further (page 444)

Practice   Complete each sentence below with a word from the box.

precise	confidence	processes	varies	advance
transferring	discouraged	application	eclipse	responsibilities

1. Maxwell was _____ from going outside by the heat.

2. Today I mailed my _____ for enrolling in a local music school.

3. The measurements need to be _____ so that the frame will fit the picture.

4. The amount of produce needed _____ depending on the recipe.

5. Niki reached out to _____ her pawn and knocked over her queen.

6. My _____ include sweeping the kitchen and taking out the trash.

7. Whenever he sits at the piano, Cameron is filled with

   _____.

8. As I am _____ this dirt to the pot, will you hold the plant?

9. Orlando looked through a special lens to view the _____.

10. There are a number of _____ involved in turning oil into gasoline.

Apply | Write a vocabulary word next to the group of words that have a similar meaning.

11. changes; alters; diverse _____

12. procedures; steps; moves _____

13. sureness; courage; self-reliance _____

14. further; promote; support _____

15. clear; accurate; explicit _____

16. sending; carrying; conveying _____

17. hindered; prevented; deterred _____

18. duties; obligations; burdens _____

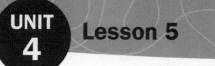

Research Report: Biography

Think

Audience: Who will read your biography?

_____

Purpose: What is your reason for writing a biography?

_____

Prewriting

Use this time line to plan your biography. Remember that a biography can cover a person's entire life, or just an important period in that person's life. Use a separate piece of paper to add more boxes if necessary.

Subject of Time Line: _____

Date   Event

_____   _____

                 _____

_____   _____

                 _____

_____   _____

                 _____

_____   _____

                 _____

Revising Use this checklist to revise your research.

- ☐ Have you checked resources like magazines, Web sites, interviews, and videos or DVDs?
- ☐ Do you have enough information to create an informative research report?
- ☐ Are the events in your time line listed in chronological order?
- ☐ Are there cause-and-effect relationships between events in your subject's life?
- ☐ Have you decided whether you will write about your subject's entire life or focus on a single event?
- ☐ Did you rewrite the information you found in your own words?

Editing/Proofreading Use this checklist to correct mistakes.

- ☐ Did you include bibliographic information for each source?
- ☐ Did you use quotation marks if you needed to quote someone's exact words?
- ☐ Did you check the spellings of proper names or specialized words against the original source?
- ☐ Did you check proper nouns and quotations to make sure they are capitalized correctly?

Publishing Use this checklist to see if you are ready to begin writing your report.

- ☐ Is the information you have found organized so that your report will have a beginning, middle, and end?
- ☐ Have you chosen a point of view for your report?

Name _____   Date _____

Spelling

Focus
• **Root words** were formed from words of other languages, such as Greek and Latin. Understanding and identifying root words and their meanings can help you spell many new words. Here are some roots in the spelling words and their meanings:

loc = "place"; *fac* = "make" or "do"; *graph* = "write"; *pop* = "people"; *vac* = "empty"; *photo* = "light"; *man* = "hand"; *bene* = "well," or "good"; *aut* or *auto* = "self," or "same"; *geo* = "earth"

Practice   **Fill in the root word and write the resulting spelling word on the line.**
Use each spelling word only once.

1. dis + _____ + ate =   _____

2. manu + _____ + ture =   _____

3. _____ + ic =   _____

4. _____ + ular =   _____

5. e + _____ + uate =   _____

6. _____ + ate =   _____

7. auto + _____ =   _____

8. _____ + tory =   _____

9. _____ + graphy =   _____

10. _____ + ulation =   _____

11. _____ + ation =   _____

12. _____ + ation =   _____

13. _____ + ulated =   _____

Word List
1. geography
2. dislocate
3. manufacture
4. locality
5. evacuate
6. allocate
7. benefactor
8. graphic
9. populated
10. photograph
11. location
12. vacate
13. popular
14. vacant
15. population
16. graphite
17. vacancy
18. factory
19. vacation
20. autograph

14. _____ + ancy =   _____

15. al + _____ + ate =   _____

16. _____ + ality =   _____

17. _____ + ular =   _____

18. bene + _____ + tor =   _____

19. _____ + ite =   _____

20. _____ + ant =   _____

Apply **Write the spelling word that is represented by the following root word meaning combinations.**

Example: at a distance + to see = *television*

21. hand + to make + *ture* =   _____

22. self + to write =   _____

23. light + to write =   _____

24. well or good + to make + *tor* = _____

25. earth + to write + *y* =   _____

Choose the word that does *not* share the same main root word as the other two and write it on the line.

26. evacuate, populated, vacant   _____

27. locality, allocate, factory   _____

28. graphite, geography, evacuate   _____

29. photograph, allocate, graphite _____

30. popular, vacancy, population   _____

31. graphic, graphite, vacate   _____

32. location, locality, vacation   _____

33. manufacture, benefactor, location _____

34. vacant, graphite, autograph   _____

35. populated, dislocate, popular   _____

Name _____ Date _____

Subject and Verb Agreement, Run-on Sentences, and Fragments

Focus The verb used in a sentence must agree with the subject.

- Add -s or -es to present tense verbs when they are singular.

- He **waits** at the table for his lunch.

- Do not add s or es to present tense verbs when they are plural or used with I or you.

- They **wait** at the table. I **wait** at the table. You **wait** at the table.

- **Run-on sentences** are two or more complete sentences written as though they are one.

- **Fragments** are groups of words that do not express a complete thought. A fragment is missing a subject, a predicate, or both.

Practice Read each pair of sentences below. Place a check mark next to the sentence that has subject and verb agreement. Also, identify each as Run-on (R), Fragment (F), or Complete (C).

1. _____ I stays with my aunt on Saturday my Grandfather on Sunday.

   _____ I stay with my aunt on Saturday my Grandfather on Sunday.

2. _____ Lisbeth and her sister throw a big party each year on the Fourth of July.

   _____ Lisbeth and her sister throws a big party each year on the Fourth of July.

3. _____ Smells funny.

   _____ Smell funny.

4. _____ Wendy and Ramona leaves on Monday Ronnie is never leaving.

   _____ Wendy and Ramona leave on Monday Ronnie is never leaving.

Rewrite each sentence, correcting subject-verb agreement and, if necessary, making it a complete sentence.

5. Paul go to the store his friends stays home.

_____

6. Because our family like pie.

_____

7. After Julius wents to the tennis match.

_____

8. The gas station, down the street, are closed today.

_____

9. The child play in the backyard the parents prepares for the celebration.

_____

10. Tony sing beautifully.

_____

11. Shirley and Loretta always agrees Ward and James never does.

_____

12. Walks as fast as I can.

_____

13. Our turtles loves taking baths our gerbil take sand baths.

_____

14. My sister, who live in Chicago, move to a different apartment every year.

_____

15. All the fishermen sail away they'll come back with nets full of fish.

_____

Name _____ **Date** _____

Words with Latin Roots

Focus **Latin roots** are common in the English language. Identifying and understanding Latin roots can help you define difficult and unfamiliar words. When you know the meaning of a root, you can figure out the meanings of many words that contain that root.

Practice The following words with Latin roots were taken from "Buffalo Hunt." Each word is followed by the root word and its definition. Think of other words that use each Latin root and write them on the line.

1. supported

port: carry _____

2. described

scrib: write _____

3. dependent

pend: hang _____

4. signal

sign: mark _____

5. sufficient

fic: make _____

Apply The following groups of words all have the same Latin roots. Circle the root that each word has in common. Then examine each word carefully and think of its definition. You may need to look up some words in a dictionary or thesaurus. Think about what the definitions have in common. Then write what you think each root means.

6. structure, reconstruction, destruction, instruct

   The Latin root is **struct.** What does **struct** mean? _____

7. tribute, contribute, tributary, attribute

   The Latin root is **trib.** What does **trib** mean? _____

8. reflex, flexible, flexor

   The Latin root is **flex.** What does **flex** mean? _____

9. dentist, dental, dentistry

   The Latin root is **dent.** What does **dent** mean? _____

10. narrate, narrator, narrative

   The Latin root is **narr.** What does **narr** mean? _____

Word Structure • *Skills Practice 2*

Name _____ Date _____

Selection Vocabulary

Focus

legends (lej'·əndz) *n.* plural of **legend:** a story passed down through the years that many people believe but that is not entirely true (page 465)

sacred (sā'·krid) *adj.* regarded as deserving respect (page 465)

stampede (stam·pēd') *v.* to cause a sudden, wild running of a frightened herd of animals (page 467)

banners (ban'·ûrz) *n.* plural of **banner:** a piece of cloth that has a design and sometimes writing on it (page 471)

lurking (lûr'·king) *adj.* lying hidden and quiet, preparing to attack (page 472)

procession (prə·sesh'·ən) *n.* a group of people moving forward in a line or in a certain order (page 472)

elders (el'·dərs) *n.* plural of **elder:** a person who is older (page 474)

cow (kou) *n.* the fully grown female of some large mammals such as buffaloes, elephants, and whales (page 478)

ladles (lā'·dəlz) *n.* plural of **ladle:** a spoon with a long handle and a bowl shaped like a cup. It is used to scoop up liquids (page 481)

pitched (pitchd) *v.* past tense of **pitch:** to set up (page 482)

Practice   Circle the word in parentheses that best fits each sentence.

1. Our (legends/elders) gave us advice about the future.

2. Melissa created colorful (reservations/banners) for the game.

3. The loud thunder started a (stampede/lurking) of the wild horses.

4. Gabriela read about the (procession/legends) of the ancient people.

5. Jesse quickly (pitched/deserted) the tent before it rained.

6. There were (banners/ladles) by every pot of soup.

7. These old books are (sacred/lurking) to our family.

8. (Lurking/Elders) in the trees, the snake waited for its prey to come.

9. The female elephant lost track of her pack, but the (cow/banners) soon found them.

10. The (procession/stampede) traveled through the city square as the entire town watched.

Apply Write *T* in the blank if the sentence for the vocabulary word is correct. Write *F* if the sentence is false. For every *F* answer, write the vocabulary word that fits the definition.

11. *Elders* are stories passed down through the years that

    many people believe but that are not entirely true. _____

    _____

12. *Ladles* are pieces of cloth with a design and sometimes writing

    on them. _____ _____

13. *Pitched* means "to set up." _____ _____

14. A *procession* is a sudden, wild running of a frightened herd

    of animals. _____ _____

15. When someone is *lurking,* he or she is lying hidden and quiet,

    as if preparing to attack. _____ _____

Name _____ **Date** _____

Recording Concept Information

**As I read each selection, this is what I added to
my understanding of the unit theme Going West.**

- "Buffalo Hunt" by Russell Freedman

  _____

  _____

- "The Journal of Wong Ming-Chung" by Lawrence Yep

  _____

  _____

- "Bill Pickett: Rodeo-Ridin' Cowboy" by Andrea Pinkney

  _____

  _____

- "Ghost Towns of the American West" by Raymond Bial

  _____

  _____

- "McBroom the Rainmaker" by Sid Fleischman

  _____

  _____

Knowledge about Going West

- This is what I know about going west before reading the unit.

_____

_____

_____

_____

_____

_____

- These are some things about going west that I would like to talk about and understand better.

_____

_____

_____

_____

_____

_____

Reminder: I should read this page again when I get to the end of the unit to see how much my ideas about going west have changed.

Name _____ Date _____

Ideas about Going West

Of the ideas discussed in class about going west, these are the ones I found most interesting.

_____

_____

_____

_____

_____

_____

_____

_____

_____

_____

_____

_____

_____

_____

_____

Ideas about Going West (continued)

Write down the ideas you found most interesting about the selection "The Journal of Wong Ming-Chung." Discuss your ideas with the class.

_____

_____

_____

_____

_____

_____

_____

_____

_____

_____

_____

_____

_____

_____

_____

_____

_____

Name _____ Date _____

Describing Two Objects

Think   **Audience: Who** will read your description?

_____

Purpose: What do you want your description to do?

_____

Prewriting   **Visualize the objects you want to describe. This method will help you focus on the most important details. Your description should be vivid and detailed. Remember to use descriptions that appeal to the five senses. Use the following graphic organizer to help you start your descriptive writing.**

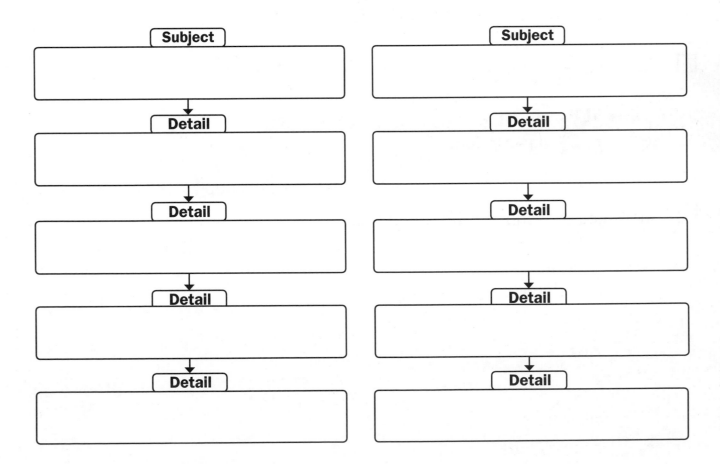

Revising

Use this checklist to revise your description.

☐ Did you include enough concrete sensory details?

☐ Are your details grouped in a way that makes sense?

☐ Have you chosen vivid and descriptive words?

☐ Have you used similes or metaphors?

☐ Will your audience know what you are describing?

Editing/Proofreading

Use this checklist to edit your description.

☐ Do the verb tenses you used make sense?

☐ Have you correctly used appositives?

☐ Have you checked your description for spelling errors?

☐ Have you used correct punctuation and capitalization?

Publishing

Use this checklist to publish your description.

☐ Write neatly or type on a computer to create a final copy.

☐ Share your description with other students.

Name _____   Date _____

Spelling

Focus

- **Homophones** are words that sound the same but have different spellings and different meanings. The following word pairs are examples of homophones.
  clause, claws   *wade, weighed*
  stationary, stationery

- Understanding and identifying **Latin roots** and their meanings can help you define and spell difficult and unfamiliar words. Here are some of the Latin roots in the spelling words and their meanings: ***terr*** = "land" or "earth"; ***ver*** = "truth"; ***tain*** and ***ten*** = "hold"

Practice   **On the line, write the homophone from the spelling list after its brief definition.**

1. part of a sentence   _____

2. animal or bird nails   _____

3. flash of light in the sky   _____

4. making less heavy   _____

5. across the ocean   _____

6. watches over   _____

7. paper for writing letters   _____

8. not moving   _____

9. walk through shallow water   _____

10. measured the heaviness of   _____

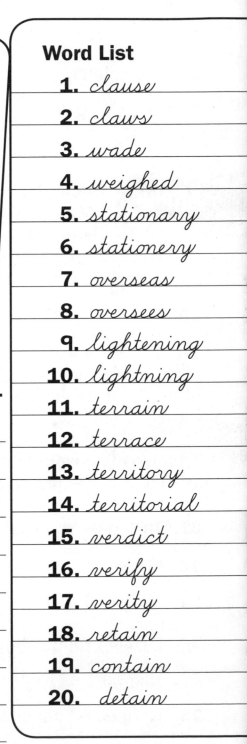

Word List
1. clause
2. claws
3. wade
4. weighed
5. stationary
6. stationery
7. overseas
8. oversees
9. lightening
10. lightning
11. terrain
12. terrace
13. territory
14. territorial
15. verdict
16. verify
17. verity
18. retain
19. contain
20. detain

Using the Latin roots provided, write the spelling words that are formed when the Latin root is added. Use each spelling word only once.

terr   *tain*

11. _____ace   _____   **14.** re_____   _____

12. _____itorial   _____   **15.** de_____   _____

13. _____itory   _____   **16.** con_____   _____

Apply Circle the misspellings, or incorrect homophones, in the sentences below. Write the misspelled words correctly on the lines provided. If there are no misspelled words in a sentence, write *correct*.

17. A flash of lightening lit up the sky.   _____

18. That cat has sharp clause.   _____

19. The letter was written on fine stationary.   _____

20. The soldier had been oversees for a year.   _____

If the spelling word in the sentence is misspelled, write the correct spelling of the word on the line. If it is correct, write *correct*.

21. The covered wagon traveled over rough turrain.   _____

22. Please do not detane us any longer.   _____

23. Has the jury decided on a verdict yet?   _____

24. Will you varify your address?   _____

25. There are all kinds of plants on the tarrace.   _____

26. What does that bowl containe?   _____

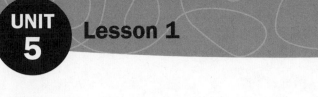

Name _____   Date _____

Verb Tense and Sentence Tense

- **Present tense** = action happening now or on a regular basis.

- **Past tense** = action that has already happened.

- **Future tense** = action that will happen. Use *will* or *shall* with the main verb.

- I **feel** a mosquito on my neck. Sean **feels** relief whenever he finishes a math test.

- Jamie **felt** bad when her favorite sports team lost.

- John **will feel** relaxed as soon as his vacation begins.

Read each sentence below. Then circle the letter of the verb tense the sentence contains.

1. The waves rolled onto the beach and swept away the sandcastle bit by bit.

   a. future tense   **b.** present tense   **c.** past tense

2. A school bus will take our class to a museum on Thursday.

   a. past tense   **b.** present tense   **c.** future tense

3. Maddy eats a peanut butter sandwich for lunch nearly every day.

   a. present tense   **b.** past tense   **c.** future tense

4. At the end of the year, Shonda will complete her second year of piano lessons.

   a. present tense   **b.** future tense   **c.** past tense

5. Yesterday, I went to the mall to buy my sister a birthday present.

   a. present tense   **b.** past tense   **c.** future tense

Apply Read the following sentences. If the verb tenses used in the sentence make sense, place a check mark on the line. If they do not make sense, rewrite the sentence using the correct tense for the underlined verb on the lines provided.

6. _____ Whenever Aunt Lucy traveled, she <u>makes</u> at least one new friend.

_____

_____

7. _____ If the city decides to widen the road, workers <u>will chop</u> down that tree.

_____

_____

8. _____ The students have planned a going-away party for Allison, who <u>moved</u> to Las Vegas tomorrow.

_____

_____

9. _____ A truck rumbled down the street, and an airplane <u>has flown</u> overhead.

_____

_____

10. _____ We will finish this lesson next week, so you <u>will need</u> to have the new book by then.

_____

_____

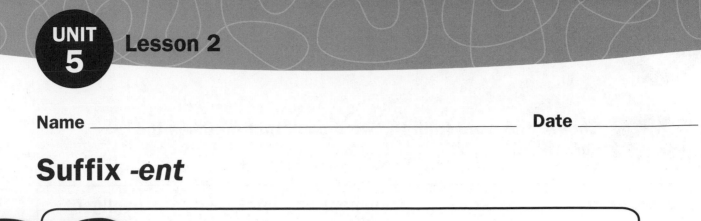

Name _____ Date _____

Suffix *-ent*

 **Focus** | The suffix *-ent* means "having the quality of." When it is added to a root word, it usually forms an adjective.

Practice | Change each boldfaced word below to form the word with the suffix *-ent* that matches the definition.

1. has the quality of **depending**

   _____

2. has the quality of **differing**

   _____

3. has the quality of **emerging**

   _____

4. has the quality of **appearing** clearly

   _____

5. has the quality of **absorbing**

   _____

Apply Choose the word from the word bank that matches the definitions.

competent	insistent	permanent	intelligent	negligent
convenient	excellent	complacent	efficient	apparent

6. nearby or easily accessible _____

7. having the quality of excelling _____

8. having the quality of competence _____

9. having the quality of permanence _____

10. having the quality of insisting _____

11. having the quality of being satisfied or pleased _____

12. having the quality of being visible or easily understood

_____

13. having the quality of being productive without being wasteful

_____

14. having the quality of being smart or having intelligence

_____

15. having the quality of being careless or showing neglect

_____

Name _____ Date _____

Selection Vocabulary

Focus

immigrants (i'·mi·grənts) *n.* plural of **immigrant:** a person who comes to live in a country in which he or she was not born (page 498)

endure (in·dûr') *v.* to put up with (page 498)

rationed (rash'·nd) *v.* past tense of **ration:** to limit to fixed portions (page 499)

burden (bûr'·dən) *n.* a difficult undertaking (page 501)

squat (skwot) *v.* to crouch or sit with the knees bent and drawn close to the body (page 503)

theory (thər'·ē) *n.* an opinion based on some evidence but not proven (page 504)

boast (bōst) *n.* a statement in which one brags (page 505)

registered (re'·jə·stərd) *v.* past tense of **register:** to officially record (page 506)

investment (in·vest'·mənt) *adj.* using money to buy something that will make more money (page 507)

raggedy (rag'·i·dē) *adj.* torn or worn-out (page 508)

Practice

Tell whether the boldfaced definition that is given for the underlined word in each sentence below is correct. Circle *Yes* or *No*.

1. Luis <u>registered</u> his boat as soon as he bought it.
   officially recorded for protection................................. Yes   No

2. My sister finally threw away her <u>raggedy</u> doll.
   worn-out ....Yes   No

3. My grandparents are <u>immigrants</u> from China. **a group of families descended from the same ancestor**.............Yes   No

4. The explorers <u>rationed</u> their food supply.
   limited to fixed portions...Yes   No

5. Our <u>investment</u> in stocks was profitable.
money used to make money .... Yes   No

6. John tried to <u>endure</u> the long wait for his turn at the park.
to put up with .... Yes   No

7. His <u>theory</u> on atoms had not yet been proven wrong.
opinion proven and accepted as law .... Yes   No

8. The <u>burden</u> of carrying the box up the stairs was overwhelming.
easily achieved .... Yes   No

9. I had to <u>squat</u> behind a bush to avoid being discovered.
to crouch or sit with the knees bent .... Yes   No

10. Jim tended to <u>boast</u> after he won his match.
to brag .... Yes   No

Apply   **Match each word to its definition on the right.**

11. investment   **a.** a difficult undertaking

12. endure   **b.** officially recorded for protection

13. registered   **c.** money used to make money

14. rationed   **d.** to put up with

15. burden   **e.** limited to fixed portions

Name _____   Date _____

Sequence

When writers tell a story or explain a process, they must express the sequence in which events occur.

Sequence is indicated by time words and order words.

- Words such as *earlier, later, now, then, morning, day, evening,* and *night* indicate **time.**

- Words such as *first, second, last, following, next, after, during,* and *finally* indicate **order.**

Look through "The Journal of Wong Ming-Chung." Choose one of the diary entries and summarize the sequence of events on the lines provided. Be sure to include time words and order words.

Page: _____

Entry date: _____

Events in sequence: _____

_____

_____

_____

_____

_____

_____

_____

_____

Apply Think about the things you have done so far today. Make a list of those things, placing them in the proper sequence.

_____

_____

_____

_____

_____

Now, write a paragraph describing your day so far. Use time words and order words to express the sequence of events in your day.

_____

_____

_____

_____

_____

_____

Name _____ **Date** _____

Formulating Questions and Problems

A good question or problem to investigate:

_____

_____

_____

_____

Why this is an interesting question or problem:

_____

_____

_____

_____

Some other things I wonder about this question or problem:

_____

_____

_____

_____

Formulating Questions and Problems (continued)

My investigation group's question or problem:

_____

_____

_____

_____

What our investigation will contribute to the rest of the class:

_____

_____

_____

_____

Some other things I wonder about this question or problem:

_____

_____

_____

_____

Name _____ Date _____

Poetry: Free Verse

Think   Audience: **Who** will read your poem?

_____

Purpose: **What** do you want your readers to think about your poem?

_____

Prewriting   Once you have chosen a subject for your free-verse poem, use the graphic organizer below to get started. Fill in the ovals surrounding the topic with details about your subject. These details can be descriptions, thoughts, ideas, or anything else that comes to mind.

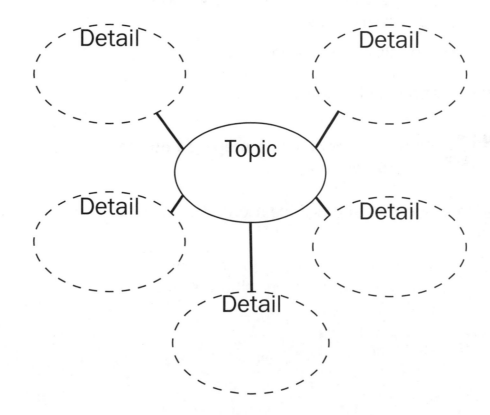

Revising

Use this checklist to revise your poem.

☐ Did you use a thesaurus to choose vivid and precise descriptive words?

☐ Is every word and phrase in your poem necessary?

☐ Did you use figurative language to create strong images and ideas?

Editing/Proofreading

Use this checklist to correct mistakes.

☐ Have you checked you poem for misused verbs, pronouns, and modifiers?

☐ Did you use correct verb tenses?

☐ Did you use spaces and line breaks in your poem to show the reader when to pause?

☐ Did you use capitalization in a consistent way?

☐ Did you use end punctuation correctly?

Publishing

Use this checklist to prepare your poem for publication.

☐ Rewrite your poem neatly or type it on a computer to create a final copy.

☐ Practice reading your poem until you are confident you know the rhythm. Read your poem aloud to the class.

Name _____   **Date** _____

Spelling

Focus

The suffixes **-ant** and **-ent** both mean "one who" when added to words to form nouns. The suffixes mean "having the quality of" when added to words to form adjectives.

Practice

Add the suffix -ant or -ent to the following word parts and write the resulting spelling words on the lines.

1. import _____   _____

2. pati _____   _____

3. stud _____   _____

4. pollut _____   _____

5. resid _____   _____

6. conveni _____   _____

7. domin _____   _____

8. disinfect _____   _____

9. dist _____   _____

10. correspond _____   _____

11. fragr _____   _____

12. independ _____   _____

13. observ _____   _____

14. toler _____   _____

15. perman _____   _____

Word List

1. independent
2. excellent
3. resident
4. superintendent
5. correspondent
6. patient
7. permanent
8. convenient
9. student
10. insistent
11. important
12. observant
13. disinfectant
14. distant
15. dominant
16. relevant
17. fragrant
18. pollutant
19. abundant
20. tolerant

16. excell_____ _____

17. abund_____ _____

18. relev_____ _____

19. insist_____ _____

20. superintend_____ _____

Apply
Circle the misspelled words in the sentences and write them correctly in the spaces provided.

21. The food was abundant and excellant. _____

22. The disinfectent was not fragrant. _____

23. An observent student found the mistake. _____

24. She is the superintendant in a distant district. _____

25. The teacher praised the patient studant. _____

26. Are you a permanant resident of this state? _____

27. The news correspondent traveled to distent lands. _____

28. The independant patient wanted to leave the hospital. _____

29. A certain pollutent is abundant in our area. _____

30. The importent builder listened to the insistent residents. _____

Name _____ Date _____

Sentence Types

- A **declarative** sentence makes a statement. It always ends with a period.

- My best friend is Reynaldo.

- An **interrogative** sentence asks a question. It ends with a question mark.

- Did you see the goal Ana made?

- An **imperative** sentence gives a command or makes a request. It usually ends with a period.

- Please call the police.

- An **exclamatory** sentence expresses a strong feeling. It ends with an exclamation point.

- That was a yummy dessert!

Practice **Add the correct end punctuation to these sentences.**

1. Do you know anything about Alaska
2. The United States bought Alaska from Russia in 1867
3. Henry Seward was the Secretary of State at that time, and he arranged to purchase Alaska for $7 million
4. People called the territory "Seward's Folly" because they thought it cost too much money
5. An amazing thing happened five years later
6. The discovery of gold started a rush to Alaska
7. Can you name two important energy sources also found there

Apply Label the following sentences as declarative, interrogative, imperative, or exclamatory.

8. Where is Julio taking those boxes? _____

9. Stay with Trevor until I get back from the store. _____

10. While Mr. James jogged, his wife read at the library. _____

11. Stop making that noise! _____

12. Listen as I tell you about my childhood. _____

13. You should eat five servings of produce each day. _____

14. Does Emily know when the next train is scheduled to arrive?

_____

15. Please carry this message to Ms. Hampton. _____

Name _____ Date _____

Word Relationships

Focus As you read, you will notice that many words relate to each other because they are about the same topic. These **word relationships** can give you clues about the meanings of unfamiliar words.

Practice The words in each group below are related. Determine how the words in each line are related, and write a description of the relationship on the lines below. Use a dictionary if you need help.

1. deck   sail   oar   rudder

_____

2. sidewalk   pathway   trail   lane

_____

3. forest   leaves   trunk   bark

_____

4. English   Spanish   French   Portuguese

_____

5. roof   shingles   plywood   gutter

_____

6. bat   catcher's mitt   helmet   cleats

_____

Apply   Search the selection "Bill Pickett: Rodeo-Ridin' Cowboy." Choose five words from the selection that are related to one another. Write the words on the lines below, and then describe their relationship in column two.

7. _____   **Relationship:** _____

_____   _____

_____   ⟶   _____

_____   _____

8. _____   **Relationship:** _____

_____   _____

_____   ⟶   _____

_____   _____

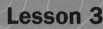

Name _____   Date _____

Selection Vocabulary

Focus

enslaved (in·slāvd') *adj.* past tense of **enslave:** to hold in slavery (page 519)

bundled (bun'·dəld) *v.* past tense of **bundle:** to tie or wrap together (page 519)

trek (trek) *n.* a long, slow journey (page 519)

prospering (pros'·pər·ing) *v.* doing extremely well (page 520)

straddled (stra'·dəld) *v.* past tense of **straddle:** to sit with one's legs on each side of an object (page 522)

rickety (ri'·ki·tē) *adj.* likely to fall or break (page 522)

challenge (chal'·ənj) *n.* a call to take part in a difficult task or contest (page 526)

lasso (la'·sō) *v.* to catch an animal using a long rope with a loop (page 527)

association (ə·sō'·sē·ā'·shən) *n.* a group of people joined together for a common purpose (page 528)

stunt (stunt) *n.* an act of skill or strength (page 528)

Practice   Circle the correct letter to answer each question below.

1. Which is an example of the word *prospering?*
   a. a store where no one shops
   b. a store where everyone shops

2. Which is an example of a person who would use a *lasso?*
   a. someone who works in a hospital
   b. someone who works on a ranch

3. Which is an example of something that is *rickety?*
   a. a floor with holes in it
   b. a sturdy table

4. Which is an example of a *stunt?*
   a. lifting a small dog
   b. lifting five hundred pounds

5. Which is an example of something that is *bundled?*
   a. a stack of newspapers tied with a string
   b. a winter coat hanging in the closet

6. Which is an example of a *challenge?*
   a. cooking a meal for one hundred people
   b. calling a friend on the phone

7. Which is an example of an *association?*
   a. two friends going to a movie
   b. neighbors meeting to clean up litter every month

8. Which is an example of a *trek?*
   a. a cross-country trip
   b. a walk around the block

9. Which is an example of someone *enslaved?*
   a. a person forced to work for someone with no compensation
   b. a person who chooses to work for someone for compensation

10. Which is an example of something being *straddled?*
    a. riding a horse
    b. sitting on a chair

Apply

Review the vocabulary words and definitions from *Bill Pickett: Rodeo-Ridin' Cowboy*. On a separate sheet of paper, write five sentences that each use at least one of the vocabulary words from this lesson.

Name _____ Date _____

Fact and Opinion

Focus Good writers use both facts and opinions in their writing. A good reader can tell one from the other.

- **Facts** are details that can be proven true or false.
- **Opinions** are what people think. They cannot be proven true or false.

Practice Skim "Bill Pickett: Rodeo-Ridin' Cowboy" for examples in which the author states facts and opinions. Write the page number, identify each example as a fact or opinion, and write the example. Be sure to find examples of both.

1. Page: _____ Fact or opinion? _____

Example: _____

2. Page: _____ Fact or opinion? _____

Example: _____

_____

3. Page: _____ Fact or opinion? _____

Example: _____

4. Page: _____ Fact or opinion? _____

Example: _____

_____

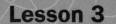
Apply **Read each sentence below and tell whether it is a fact or an opinion.**

5. Covered wagons were the best mode of transportation for pioneers. _____

6. As Americans began to explore the land out west, they found it inhabited by Native Americans. _____

7. Lewis and Clark were among the first to journey west on a scientific expedition. _____

8. A new life in a new land was worth the slow, steady trek pioneers made across country. _____

9. When Bill Pickett's two cousins came to visit, they bragged about their life on the trail. _____

10. A cowboy's life was a good life. _____

Explorers, hunters, naturalists, cowboys, and other adventurers traveled west. Select one of these adventurers and write a paragraph about his or her travels. You may want to do some research to get factual information. Include both facts and opinions in your paragraph.

_____

_____

_____

_____

_____

_____

Comprehension Skill • *Skills Practice 2*

Name _____ **Date** _____

Making Conjectures

Our question or problem:

_____

_____

_____

_____

_____

Conjecture (my first theory or explanation):

_____

_____

_____

_____

_____

_____

_____

_____

_____

_____

As you collect information, your conjecture will change. Return to this page to record your new theories or explanations about your question or problem.

Establishing Investigation Needs

My group's question or problem:

_____

_____

_____

_____

_____

Knowledge Needs—Information I need to find or figure out in order to investigate the question or problem:

A. _____

B. _____

C. _____

D. _____

E. _____

Source	Useful?	How?
Encyclopedias		
Books		
Magazines		
Newspapers		
Videotapes, filmstrips, and so on		
Television		
Interviews, observations		
Museums		
Other:		

Inquiry • *Skills Practice 2*

Name _____ Date _____

Poetry: Lyric

Think **Audience: Who** will read your lyrical poem?

_____

Purpose: What do you want readers to think about your poem?

_____

Prewriting Lyrical poetry expresses an author's feelings about the poem's subject. Use the graphic organizer below to explore the emotions—both positive and negative—that you have about the topic you have chosen for your poem.

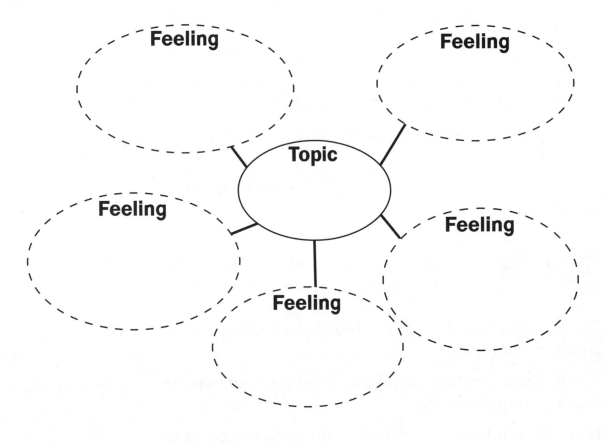

Revising — Use this checklist to revise your poem.

☐ Have you replaced bland adjectives, adverbs, and verbs with ones that are vivid and descriptive?

☐ If your poem rhymes, did you follow a consistent pattern throughout the poem?

☐ Do the words and phrases in your poem create a musical rhythm?

☐ Does your poem have one main focus or idea?

☐ Does your poem show your true feelings about the topic?

Editing/Proofreading — Use the following checklist to correct mistakes.

☐ Did you use commas correctly throughout your poem?

☐ Does your poem have any misspelled homophones?

☐ Did you use a consistent method for capitalization and punctuation throughout your poem?

☐ Have you checked for misused verbs, pronouns, or modifiers?

☐ Have you used standard proofreading marks to edit misspelled homophones?

Publishing — Use this checklist to prepare your poem for publication.

☐ Rewrite your poem neatly or type it on a computer to create a final copy.

☐ Add illustrations to your poem, or create a collage about your poem's topic.

☐ Present your poem by reading it aloud to the class or adding it to a class anthology.

Name _____ Date _____

Spelling

Focus
- **Compound words** consist of two smaller words that have been combined to form one larger word. These two words keep the same spelling in the compound word.
- **Homographs** are words that are spelled the same, but have different meanings, different word origins, and sometimes, different pronunciations.

Practice The following spelling words are missing one of their base words. Write the whole compound words on the lines.

1. _____ground   _____

2. over_____   _____

3. _____stand   _____

4. _____light   _____

5. _____time   _____

6. blue_____   _____

7. stock _____   _____

8. _____foot   _____

9. _____while   _____

10. motor_____   _____

Word List
1. bluebonnet
2. stockyards
3. newsstand
4. sunlight
5. campground
6. meanwhile
7. motorcycle
8. springtime
9. barefoot
10. overhead
11. invalid
12. launch
13. minute
14. school
15. spruce
16. capital
17. refuse
18. compound
19. reserved
20. cardinal

On the line, write the homograph from the spelling list after its brief definition.

11. to say no   _____

12. person who is disabled   _____

13. to put in motion   _____

14. very small   _____

15. group of fish   _____

16. to make neat or trim   _____

17. money or assets   _____

18. enclosed area with buildings   _____

19. of greatest importance   _____

20. quiet or shy   _____

Apply

On the line, write the spelling word from the list that contains one of the base words in the following compound words

21. flashlight _____

26. threadbare _____

22. headache _____

27. campsite _____

23. tricycle _____

28. anytime _____

24. awhile _____

29. backyards _____

25. blueberry _____

30. newspaper _____

Name _____ Date _____

Colons and Semicolons

Focus

- **Colons** (:) are used to introduce lists, to separate the minutes and hours of a precise time, and at the end of a business letter's salutation.

- **Semicolons** (;) are used to join independent clauses in a sentence and to help separate clauses joined by some adverbs. Use a semicolon when conjunctions like *and* or *but* are not used.

Practice Each sentence below contains a colon or a semicolon. If the correct punctuation mark was used, write *C* in the blank. If the incorrect punctuation mark was used, write *I* in the blank.

1. _____ My brother thought I took his favorite book: he was wrong.

2. _____ Hannah's day always consists of the following meals: breakfast, lunch, and dinner.

3. _____ To whom it may concern;

4. _____ Our match starts at exactly 10;15.

5. _____ Earthquakes are caused by movement deep underground; however, they can still be felt at the surface.

6. _____ Aunt Millie always brings these things when she visits; baked goods, a couple of books, and a big smile.

7. _____ Juan just returned from Alaska; he's heading to Montana next.

8. _____ Every Wednesday at 4:00 I have dance lessons.

Apply Add colons and/or semicolons where they are needed in the following sentences.

9. Marcus searched for blueberries on his hike he did not find any.

10. The race began at 9 15 my family was there watching from the sidelines.

11. Please try to bring one of the following items a tablecloth, eating utensils, napkins, or cleaning supplies.

12. Shawna thought she had caught a lightning bug when she opened her hand, it was gone.

13. Earth has four oceans the Pacific, the Atlantic, the Indian, and the Arctic.

14. Tell Li to memorize the code she'll get locked out if she doesn't remember it.

15. Go to the fridge and grab the milk, three eggs, and some cheese we're going to make an omelet.

16. Last night at 7 30, Kyle received a call from overseas however, it was a wrong number.

Synonyms and Antonyms

- **Synonyms** are words with the same, or nearly the same, meaning. For example, *giant, huge,* and *massive* are all synonyms.

- **Antonyms** are words with opposite or nearly opposite meanings. An antonym for *empty* is *full,* and an antonym for *dull* is *exciting.*

Practice The first word of each pair below is from "Ghost Towns of the American West." Write *S* on the line if the second word is a synonym. Write *A* on the line if it is an antonym.

1. _____ communities neighborhoods

2. _____ lonely isolated

3. _____ vanished appeared

4. _____ general specific

5. _____ fragile delicate

6. _____ rubbish garbage

7. _____ vacant occupied

8. _____ cheerful upbeat

9. _____ surrounded enclosed

10. _____ longing hoping

Apply

For each word below, write an antonym on the first line and a synonym on the second line. Use a dictionary and thesaurus if you need help.

11. suspicious

Antonym: _____ Synonym: _____

12. removed

Antonym: _____ Synonym: _____

13. fake

Antonym: _____ Synonym: _____

14. entire

Antonym: _____ Synonym: _____

15. professional

Antonym: _____ Synonym: _____

16. nervous

Antonym: _____ Synonym: _____

17. created

Antonym: _____ Synonym: _____

18. foreign

Antonym: _____ Synonym: _____

Name _____ Date _____

Selection Vocabulary

Focus

longed (longd) *v.* past tense of **long**: to want very much; yearn (page 548)

evidence (e'·və·dəns) *n.* proof of something (page 548)

tattered (tat'·ərd) *adj.* torn into shreds (page 549)

trough (trôf) *n.* a long narrow container that holds water or food for animals (page 549)

territory (ter'·i·tôr'·ē) *n.* a large area or region of land (page 549)

centuries (sen'·chə·rēs) *n.* plural of **century**: a period of one hundred years (page 549)

minerals (min'·ər·əls) *n.* plural of **mineral**: a substance found in nature that is not an animal or plant. Salt, coal, and gold are minerals. (page 550)

prosperity (pros·per'·i·tē) *n.* success, wealth, or good fortune (page 550)

traces (trās'·ez) *n.* plural of **trace**: a small bit or sign left behind showing that something was there (page 551)

inhabitants (in·ha'·bə·tənts) *n.* plural of **inhabitant**: a person or animal that lives in a place (page 557)

Practice | Circle the letter of the word that correctly completes each sentence.

1. The only _____ of the party were a few crumbs and empty cups sitting on the table.

   a. minerals   **b.** traces   **c.** inhabitants

2. The bottom edge of the curtain was _____ where the cat had been playing with it.

   a. longed   **b.** traces   **c.** tattered

3. The Abu-Jabars have lived in the _____ since the 1930s.

   a. inhabitants   **b.** territory   **c.** prosperity

4. The mining company owns all the _____ that they dig out of the mountain.

    a. minerals   **b.** evidence   **c.** trough

5. For _____, kings and queens ruled much of the world.

    a. prosperity   **b.** inhabitants   **c.** centuries

6. A _____ filled with water ran along one entire side of the barn.

    a. minerals   **b.** trough   **c.** longed

7. The detective quickly saw that all the _____ was fake.

    a. traces   **b.** minerals   **c.** evidence

8. The McKenzies' _____ came from owning a store.

    a. prosperity   **b.** minerals   **c.** territory

9. The _____ of the rain forest know how to use the land's resources.

    a. inhabitants   **b.** territory   **c.** traces

10. After several weeks away from home, Sara _____ to see her family.

    a. prosperity   **b.** traces   **c.** longed

 Apply   **Write the vocabulary word that best matches the underlined word or phrase in the sentences below.**

11. A dozen hogs lined up to eat at the <u>long, narrow container</u> filled with grain.

_____

12. For <u>hundreds of years</u> the castle has stood towering over the valley.

_____

13. During the first week, I <u>wanted</u> to be back at my old school.

_____

14. The only way to <u>success</u> is through hard work. _____

Name _____ Date _____

Poetry: Quatrain

Think | **Audience: Who** will read your quatrain?

_____

Purpose: What do you want your readers to think about your quatrain?

_____

Prewriting | Including sensory details in your poem will make its images more vivid and complex. Use this graphic organizer to plan your quatrain.

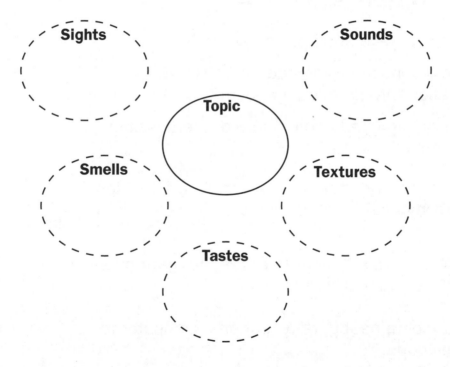

Revising
Use this checklist to revise your quatrain.

☐ Do you use a correct rhyming pattern for your quatrain?

☐ Have you used a thesaurus or rhyming dictionary to choose unique and descriptive words?

☐ Do your words and sensory details convey the mood of your poem?

☐ Does your poem have a consistent rhyming pattern?

☐ Do the words, phrases, and punctuation create a noticeable rhythm?

Editing/Proofreading
Use this following checklist to correct mistakes.

☐ Does your poem have any spelling errors?

☐ Did you use a consistent method for capitalization and punctuation throughout your poem?

☐ Have you correctly used one or more of the possible rhyming patterns?

☐ Have you correctly used participial phrases, transition words, and commas?

Publishing
Use this checklist to prepare your poem for publication.

☐ Rewrite your poem neatly, or type it on a computer to create a final copy.

☐ Use paste-up to add graphics representing the sensory details in your poem.

☐ Present your poem by reading it aloud to the class, adding it to a class anthology, or entering it in a poetry contest.

Name _____ Date _____

Spelling

- **Synonyms** are words with the same, or nearly the same, meaning. Use synonyms to help you remember the meaning of a new word.

- A **base word family** is a family of words that share a base word. When you know the meaning of a base word, you can begin to determine the meanings of the other words in the base word family.

Word List

1. expansion
2. growth
3. opportunity
4. chance
5. fortune
6. wealth
7. gratitude
8. appreciation
9. petite
10. undersized
11. special
12. specialty
13. especially
14. include
15. inclusive
16. inclusion
17. command
18. commander
19. commandeer
20. commanding

Practice On the lines, write word pairs from the word list that are synonyms. Use a thesaurus or dictionary if you need help.

1. _____   7. _____

2. _____   8. _____

3. _____   9. _____

4. _____   10. _____

5. _____

6. _____

Complete each base word and write the resulting spelling word on the line.

11. _____ial   _____

12. _____clude   _____

13. _____mand   _____

On the line, write the base word in each spelling word on the line.

14. commandeer _____

18. inclusion _____

15. inclusive _____

19. commanding _____

16. especially _____

20. specialty _____

17. commander _____

Apply

For each word, list the spelling words that are synonyms.

enlargement

1. _____

2. _____

riches

5. _____

6. _____

thanks

3. _____

4. _____

occasion

7. _____

8. _____

Correct each underlined word and write it on the line. If the word is already correct, write correct.

9. That movie was <u>espeshully</u> good. _____

10. Do not forget to <u>include</u> a tip. _____

11. Apple pie is my aunt's <u>speshialty</u>. _____

12. They voted on his <u>incloosion</u> in their club. _____

13. I <u>comand</u> you to open the door. _____

14. The ship's <u>comander</u> fell sick. _____

Name _____ **Date** _____

Transition Words

Focus

Transition words link sentences and paragraphs to each other. They help ideas flow smoothly. Transition words make writing clearer, more accurate, and help the reader move smoothly from one idea to another.

- Transition words show time: *yesterday, the day before yesterday, this morning, today, tomorrow, tonight, this afternoon, this moment.*

- Transition words show order of occurrence: *earlier, about, as soon as, soon, finally, when, meanwhile, until, later, next, now, then, finally, last.*

- Transition words show contrast: *although, but, even, though, however, on the other hand, otherwise, still, while, yet, in contrast.*

- Use transition words to compare two things: *also, too, both, in the same way, just as, likewise, like, similarly.*

- Transition words signal additional information: *additionally, again, along with, also, and, another, besides, finally, for example, further, moreover.*

- Transition words introduce a conclusion or a summary: *as a result, finally, in conclusion, in summary, last, lastly, therefore.*

Practice

Transition words may be used for more than one purpose in a paragraph. Circle the transition words used below.

1. Both Tiana and Maya like swimming, but Maya likes to swim freestyle and Tiana prefers the butterfly stroke. Both also swim the backstroke. Yesterday they practiced all three strokes for the meet today. This morning they woke up early, had a good breakfast, and did stretching exercises. This afternoon they will each swim in two events.

Apply

2. Cross out the two transition words *least* likely to be used
for each writing assignment.

Writing Assignment	Transition Words
The end of a persuasive report	*in conclusion, yesterday, therefore, finally, underneath*
A description of a waterfall	*in summary, above, at the bottom, moreover, under*
A contrast of two books	*both, but, however, likewise, on the other hand*

3. Use transition words that show location to describe a school bus.

_____

_____

4. Use transition words that signal additional information to describe a school policy.

_____

_____

5. Use transition words that compare and contrast to describe two different pets.

_____

_____

6. Use transition words to introduce the concluding paragraph for either an imaginary school report or for one you wrote earlier this year.

_____

_____

Name _____ Date _____

Language/Word Structure and the Suffix *-ic*

Focus

Understanding **word structure** can help you discover the meanings of words. Identifying the individual parts of a word's structure can help you determine the word's meaning.

• The suffix *-ic* means "of, relating to, or possessing the characteristics of." It usually forms adjectives.

Practice

Divide each of the following words into base words, prefixes, suffixes, and other inflectional endings. Circle each word that contains the suffix *-ic* and write its definition on the line.

1. discovered _____

_____

2. unpoetic _____

_____

3. nonmetallic _____

_____

4. unrealistic _____

_____

5. exactly _____

_____

Apply   Combine each base word below with at least two word parts from the box to create five new words. Then use each new word correctly in a sentence.

ed	tion	en	dis	non	ly
less	pre	mis	ing	in	able

6. Base word: order   New word: _____

Sentence: _____

_____

7. Base word: stop   New word: _____

Sentence: _____

_____

8. Base word: use   New word: _____

Sentence: _____

_____

9. Base word: joy   New word: _____

Sentence: _____

_____

10. Base word: large   New word: _____

Sentence: _____

_____

Name _____ Date _____

Selection Vocabulary

Focus

regard (re·gärd')
n. thought or care
(page 566)

merciful (mûr'·si·fəl) *adj.* kind or
forgiving (page 566)

predict (pri'·dikt) *v.* to tell
beforehand (page 567)

accurate (ak'·yər·it) *adj.* correct;
exact (page 567)

drought (drout) *n.* a period of time
when there is very little rain or no
rain at all (page 571)

prairie (prâ'·rē) *n.* a large area
of level or rolling land with grass
and few or no trees (page 573)

desperately (des'·pə·rət·lē)
adv. hopelessly (page 573)

sowing (sō'·ing) *v.* planting
(page 575)

heaved (hēvd) *v.* past tense of
heave: to make a sound with a
lot of effort or strain (page 575)

dispositions (dis'·pə·zi'·shəns)
n. plural of **disposition**: a natural
way of acting; mood (page 576)

Practice Write the word from the word box that matches
each definition below.

1. _____ hopelessly

2. _____ kind or forgiving

3. _____ a large area of level or rolling land with
grass and few or no trees

4. _____ make a sound with a lot of effort or strain

5. _____ thought or care

6. _____ dry weather that lasts a long time

7. _____ planting

8. _____ natural ways of acting

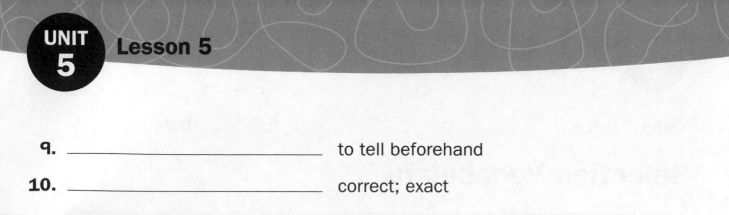

9. _____ to tell beforehand

10. _____ correct; exact

Apply **Circle the word in parentheses that best fits each sentence.**

11. Reno was (sowing/predict) seeds in the pumpkin patch.

12. She showed no regard/dispositions) for the hard work of her teammates.

13. My mother is usually (merciful/accurate) when I do something wrong.

14. The crops are dying because of the (drought/prairie).

15. Dawn is (rowdy/desperately) trying to finish her homework before bedtime.

16. The wind moves quickly across the (drought/prairie).

17. They hoped that the weather forecast was (accurate/merciful).

18. Everyone likes my brothers because they have cheerful (legends/dispositions).

Name _____ Date _____

Cause and Effect

Most stories revolve around several cause-and-effect relationships. Recognizing these relationships can help readers better understand the story.

A **cause** is why something happened.

An **effect** is what happened.

When one event causes another to happen, the events have a cause-and-effect relationship.

- A **cause** is the reason that an event happens.
- An **effect** is the result of the cause.
- Writers use words such as *because, since, therefore,* and *so* to show the reader that a cause-and-effect relationship has taken place.

Look through "McBroom the Rainmaker" and identify four effects on animals caused by the drought.

Effect: _____

Effect: _____

Effect: _____

Effect: _____

Apply   **Read the sentences below and identify the cause and effect in each one.**

1. We spent our bus money at the mall, so we had to walk home.

Effect: _____

Cause: _____

2. My dad gave me five dollars because I washed the car.

Effect: _____

Cause: _____

3. I stayed home from school because I was sick.

Effect: _____

Cause: _____

4. I slipped on the ice and broke my ankle.

Effect: _____

Cause: _____

5. My dog started barking when he heard the doorbell ring.

Effect: _____

Cause: _____

On a separate sheet of paper, write a paragraph that includes several cause-and-effect relationships. You might use one of the sentences above as the basis of your paragraph.

Name _____ Date _____

Tall Tale

Think   **Audience: Who** will read your tall tale?

_____

Purpose: What is your purpose for writing a tall tale?

_____

Prewriting   Use this graphic organizer to plan your tall tale.

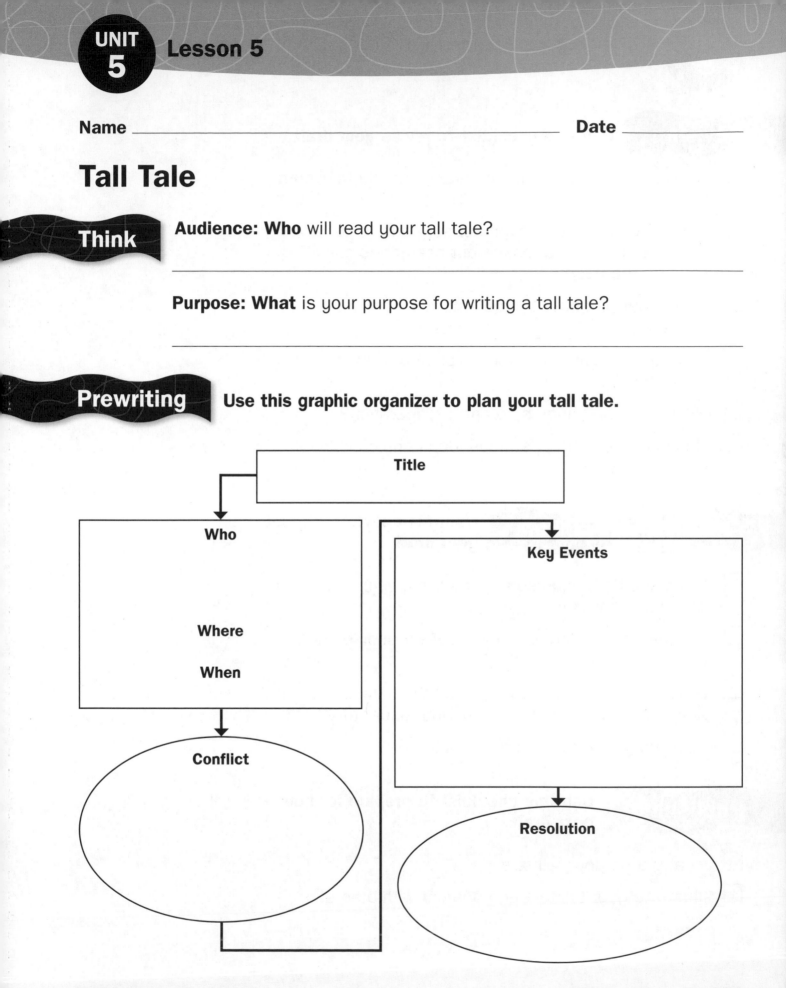

Revising   Use this checklist to revise your draft.

☐ Have you used transitional phrases to clarify events and tighten plot?

☐ Have you included enough sensory details to establish mood and make your characters come alive on the page?

☐ Does your plot have a problem, rising action, and a climax?

☐ Have you consistently used a point of view for your story?

☐ Have you used hyperbole and exaggeration?

☐ Have you deleted repetitious ideas and combined sentences?

Editing/Proofreading   Use this checklist to edit your draft.

☐ Have you correctly used appositives, verb tense, and participial phrases?

☐ Are the names you have invented for people and places humorous and silly?

☐ Have you capitalized and spelled the names of people and places consistently throughout your story?

☐ Have you used transition words to help your story flow?

Publishing   Use this checklist to prepare for your next draft.

☐ Neatly type your tall tale.

☐ Illustrate your tall tale and share it with others.

Name _____ Date _____

Spelling

Focus

- Some words end in the suffix **-ic,** which means "of, relating to, or possessing the characteristics of."

- When adding an ending that begins with a vowel, such as -er, -es, or -ed, to a word ending in a consonant and a y, change the y to an i. If a word ends with a vowel and a y, just add the ending. Do not change the y to an i if the ending is -ing.

Practice   **Add the suffix -ic to the following base words.**

1. artist + -ic = _____

2. patriot + -ic = _____

3. metal + -ic = _____

4. class + -ic = _____

5. drama + -ic = _____

6. realist + -ic = _____

7. base + -ic = _____

8. poet + -ic = _____

9. ocean + -ic = _____

10. history + -ic = _____

Word List

1. metallic
2. poetic
3. realistic
4. historic
5. classic
6. artistic
7. basic
8. dramatic
9. oceanic
10. patriotic
11. heavy
12. heavier
13. butterfly
14. butterflies
15. supply
16. supplies
17. worry
18. worried
19. mercy
20. merciful

Remove the suffixes from the following words and write the resulting spelling words on the lines.

11. worried _____

12. merciful _____

13. supplies _____

14. butterflies _____

15. heavier _____

Add the endings to the following base words and write the resulting spelling words on the lines.

16. butterfly + -es = _____

17. worry + -ed = _____

18. supply + -es = _____

19. mercy + -ful = _____

20. heavy + -er = _____

Apply   **Correct the spelling of each underlined word that is a part of a base word family and write it on the line. If the word is already correct, write correct.**

21. The action scenes were very <u>reelistic</u>.   _____

22. That rock looks almost <u>muhtallic</u>.   _____

23. She has always been <u>artistic</u>.   _____

24. The <u>osheeanic</u> breeze feels good.   _____

25. Flying the flag is <u>patriahtic</u>.   _____

26. This math is very <u>baseic</u>.   _____

Name _____ Date _____

Appositives and Participial Phrases

Appositives and participial phrases are similar to adjectives because they modify nouns or pronouns.

- An **appositive** is a noun that modifies or renames another noun or pronoun.

  My school, **DuBois Elementary,** is a fun place to learn.

- An **appositive phrase** consists of an appositive and the words that modify it.

  Uncle Chris went to France, **a country in Europe,** to study art.

- A **participial phrase** includes a verb and other words in the phrase that modify a noun or pronoun.

  The bike, **leaning quietly against the wall,** reflected sunlight onto the ground.

Practice Circle each appositive and appositive phrase in the following sentences. Underline each participial phrase.

1. That old house standing at the corner of Broad and Main will be torn down.

2. The Old West, that place of legends and adventure, has been the setting for many movies.

3. Ice cream, a popular treat throughout the world, was invented thousands of years ago.

4. Anything piled in that box can be taken to the resale shop located downtown.

5. Our teacher, Ms. Reynolds, has an aquarium filled with tropical fish.

Apply Add an appositive, an appositive phrase, or a participial phrase to each sentence below.

Example: The street was filled with cars.
The street, on which I live, was filled with cars.

6. Your brother is known around school for his talent at basketball.

_____

_____

7. Theo walked out the library's front door.

_____

_____

8. The pizza had tomato sauce, cheese, and pepperoni.

_____

_____

9. Those paintbrushes need to be cleaned.

_____

_____

10. Our trip to New York was canceled.

_____

_____

Name _____ Date _____

Prefix *im-*, Synonyms, and Antonyms

Focus

The prefix **im-** means "not." When *im-* is added to the beginning of a word, it creates an antonym of the base word. For example, the word *perfect* becomes *imperfect.*

- **Synonyms** are words with the same, or nearly the same, meaning. For example, *giant, huge,* and *massive* are all synonyms.

- **Antonyms** are words that mean with opposite, or nearly opposite, meanings. An antonym for *empty* is *full* and an antonym for *dull* is *exciting.*

Practice A Remember the prefix *in-* also means "not." You must be careful to choose the correct prefix when creating a word's antonym. For each word below, circle its correctly formed antonym.

1. Antonym for *possible:*   inpossible   impossible

2. Antonym for *correct:*   incorrect   imcorrect

3. Antonym for *mature:*   inmature   immature

4. Antonym for *patiently:*   inpatiently   impatiently

5. Antonym for *balance:*   inbalance   imbalance

6. Antonym for *capable:*   incapable   imcapable

7. Antonym for *proper:*   inproper   improper

8. Antonym for *experienced:*   inexperienced   imexperienced

9. Antonym for *frequent:*   infrequent   imfrequent

10. Antonym for *polite:*   inpolite   impolite

Practice B

Look at the word pairs listed. Write an *S* next to the word pair if they are synonyms and an *A* next to the pair if they are antonyms.

11. memorial   monument   _____

12. design   plan   _____

13. friend   enemy   _____

14. forward   backward   _____

15. thankful   grateful   _____

Apply

Not every word that begins with *im-* uses it as a prefix meaning "not." Read the words below. If the word uses *im-* as a prefix, write its base word on the line. If the word does not use *im-* as a prefix, then circle the word. Use a dictionary if you need help.

16. imperfect   Base word: _____

17. imply   Base word: _____

18. immobile   Base word: _____

19. imitation   Base word: _____

20. imagination   Base word: _____

Name _____ Date _____

Selection Vocabulary

Focus

equator (i • kwā' • tər) *n.* the imaginary line that circles Earth's center halfway between the North and South Poles (page 594)

horrified (hor' • ə • fīd) *v.* past tense of **horrify:** to cause a feeling of great fear and dread (page 595)

tropics (trop' • iks) *n.* a region of Earth that is near the equator (page 595)

biologist (bī • o' • lə • jəst) *n.* a person who studies the way in which plants and animals and other living things live and grow, and where they are found (page 596)

species (spē' • sēz) *n.* a group of animals or plants that have many characteristics in common (page 598)

macaw (mə • kô') *n.* a long-tailed parrot (page 598)

donations (dō • nā' • shəns) *n.* plural of **donation:** a gift or contribution (page 601)

designed (di • zīnd') *v.* past tense of **design:** to create (page 602)

grateful (grāt' • fəl) *adj.* full of thanks for a favor (page 603)

monument (mon' • yə •mənt) *n.* a building or statue that is made to honor a person or event (page 605)

Practice Write *T* in the blank if the sentence for the vocabulary word is correct. Write *F* if the sentence is false. For every *F* answer, write the vocabulary word that fits the definition.

1. *Donations* are gifts. _____ _____

2. The *species* is a region of Earth near the equator. _____

_____

3. When a building is *designed,* it is created. _____ _____

4. A *biologist* is something that serves to honor or keep alive a memory.

   _____ _____

5. The *tropics* is the imaginary line that circles Earth's center. _____

   _____

6. Someone who is *grateful* is thankful. _____ _____

7. A *macaw* is a type of bird. _____ _____

8. A person who is *horrified* has a great sense of fear and dread. _____

   _____

9. A *monument* is a person who studies plant and animal life. _____

   _____

10. A *species* is a group of animals or plants that have many

    characteristics in common. _____ _____

Apply **Circle the word in parentheses that best fits each sentence below.**

11. The people were (horrified/designed) by the tornado.

12. A large stone (species/monument) stands in city hall.

13. The imaginary line that divides Earth in half is called the (biologist/equator).

14. Do you know how many (species/tropics) of snakes live in the Amazon River?

15. Our school accepted (species/donations) of new books.

Name _____ **Date** _____

Author's Purpose

Focus
The author's reason for writing a story is called the **author's purpose.**

- The author's purpose can be to inform, explain, entertain, or persuade. An author can have more than one purpose for writing.
- The author's purpose affects the details, descriptions, pictures, and dialogue that are included in a story.

Practice
Reread "Founders of the Children's Rain Forest" and then answer the following questions.

1. What do you think the author's main purpose or purposes were for writing this selection?

_____

2. What makes you think this was the purpose?

_____

_____

_____

_____

3. How successful do you think the author was in this purpose?

_____

_____

_____

_____

Read the following paragraphs and write the author's purpose for each.

4. The story "Alice in Wonderland" was originally written by Lewis Carroll as a gift for a young child named Alice. The story included his own illustrations. These were very different from any of the illustrations that were done later when he expanded the story into a book-length version.

Author's purpose: _____

5. I invented a new game. You need four bases, in-line skates for all players, a soccer ball, and a bat. First, set up the bases as you would in baseball—first, second, third, and home. Then, have a pitcher throw the soccer ball to the batter. The batter tries to hit the ball with the bat. As in baseball, the batter has three strikes before he or she is out. If the batter is successful, he or she skates around the bases. Doesn't it sound like fun?

Author's purpose: _____

Apply Take some factual information that you know or have heard in the news and use it to write an opening paragraph for an entertaining story.

_____

_____

_____

_____

_____

Comprehension Skill • *Skills Practice 2*

Name _____ Date _____

Record Concept Information

As I read the selection, this is what I added to my understanding of the call of duty.

- "Founders of the Children's Rain Forest" by Phillip Hoose

_____

_____

_____

- "Jason and the Golden Fleece" by Geraldine McCaughrean

_____

_____

_____

- "The Quest for Healing" by Philip Ardagh

_____

_____

_____

- "The White Spider's Gift" by Jaime Turner

_____

_____

_____

- "The Story of Annie Sullivan: Helen Keller's Teacher" by Bernice Selden

_____

_____

_____

Knowledge about the Call of Duty

- This is what I know about the call of duty before reading the unit.

_____

_____

_____

_____

_____

- These are some things about the call of duty that I would like to talk about and understand better.

_____

_____

_____

_____

_____

Reminder: I should read this page again when I get to the end of the unit to see how much my ideas about the call of duty have changed.

Name _____ Date _____

Ideas about the Call of Duty

Of the ideas discussed in class about the call of duty, these are the ones I found most interesting.

_____

_____

_____

_____

_____

_____

_____

_____

_____

_____

_____

_____

_____

_____

Ideas about the Call of Duty (continued)

Write down the ideas you found most interesting about the selection "Founders of the Children's Rainforest." Discuss your ideas with the class.

_____

_____

_____

_____

_____

_____

_____

_____

_____

_____

_____

_____

_____

_____

_____

_____

Name _____ Date _____

Writing a Personal Letter Via the Web

Think   **Audience: Who** will read your personal letter?

_____

Purpose: What do you want to say in your personal letter?

_____

Prewriting   **Personal letters are less formal than business letters, but they should still be polite and well written. The amount of detail you will need to include depends on how much your audience already knows about the topic. Use the following lines to determine which details should be included in your letter.**

What is the topic of your personal letter?

_____

What does your audience already know about the topic?

_____

_____

_____

What do you need to tell your audience about the topic?

_____

_____

_____

Revising

Use this checklist to revise your personal letter.

☐ Does your letter contain five parts—heading, a salutation, body, closing, and your name?

☐ Did you leave out the details that your audience would have already known?

☐ Have you deleted and consolidated to eliminate wordiness?

☐ Have you checked all the helping verbs in your sentences to be sure they are necessary?

☐ Is the tone of your letter friendly and not too formal?

Editing/Proofreading

Use this checklist to make corrections.

☐ Is your personal letter formatted correctly?

☐ Did you check all capitalization, spelling, and punctuation?

☐ Did you correctly use nouns, verbs, adjectives, and adverbs?

☐ Have you entered the correct e-mail address into the address bar?

Publishing

Use this checklist to publish your personal letter.

☐ If your letter was written in a word-processing program, attach it to an e-mail message.

☐ Click the send button.

Name _____ Date _____

Spelling

Focus

- **Root words** were formed from words of other languages, such as Greek and Latin. Here are some roots in the spelling words and their meanings:
  bio = "life"   **graph** = "write"   **auto** = "self"
  dem = "people"   **crat** = "person of power; ruler"
- The prefix **im-** usually means "not."

Practice

Fill in the missing root and write the spelling word that is formed.

dem

1. _____ocracy   _____

2. _____ocratic   _____

bio

3. _____logist   _____

4. _____graphy   _____

5. _____rhythm   _____

6. _____sphere   _____

auto

7. _____crat   _____

8. _____cratic   _____

crat

9. aristo_____   _____

10. aristo_____ic   _____

Word List

1. biography
2. biologist
3. biosphere
4. biorhythm
5. democracy
6. aristocrat
7. autocrat
8. democratic
9. aristocratic
10. autocratic
11. impossible
12. impolite
13. impatient
14. immature
15. impartial
16. impassable
17. impermanent
18. impersonal
19. impractical
20. imperfect

Add the prefix *im-* to the following base words to form spelling words. Write the spelling words on the lines.

11. partial _____

12. personal _____

13. possible _____

14. permanent _____

15. polite _____

16. patient _____

17. mature _____

18. passable _____

19. perfect _____

20. practical _____

Apply   On the line, write the spelling word that is represented by the following combinations.

21. "life" + logist _____

22. "people" + ocracy _____

23. "self" + "ruler" _____

24. "life" + sphere _____

25. "people" + "ruler" + ic _____

Use the phrase to help you determine the spelling word that fits the description best, and write the word on the line.

26. not perfect _____

27. not wanting to wait _____

28. not able to be passed _____

29. not old _____

30. not polite _____

Name _____ Date _____

Helping Verbs and Linking Verbs, Subjects and Predicates

- **Helping verbs,** also known as auxiliary verbs, work with a sentence's main verb to show action.

  Constance **will** attend camp this summer.

- **Linking verbs** are state-of-being verbs that express what a subject is or is like. State-of-being verbs can also express where one is.

  That painting is beautiful.

- The **subject** is the part of the sentence that tells *who* or *what*.

  The students visited a nature preserve.

- The **predicate** describes or tells what the subject does.

  The students **visited a nature preserve.**

Practice A In the sentences below, circle the linking verbs, and underline the helping verbs. Remember that a sentence might contain more than one helping verb.

1. Mr. Thompson's feet are sore from running a marathon.

2. The builders will chop down those trees for the new mall.

3. You must join us for dinner some time.

4. The pears tasted delicious on top of the ice cream.

5. By the time water reaches your house, it will have traveled many miles.

Practice B — Circle each subject and underline each predicate in the following sentences.

6. Denzel was a role model to many children.

7. Hannah always tried to do the right thing.

8. Samir always cheered for his favorite team, but he always respected the opposing team.

9. The dog and the cat drank from the same bowl.

10. Kathy and Gary were looking forward to the celebration on Saturday.

Apply — Write two sentences for each verb. Use the verb as an action verb in the first sentence and a linking verb in the second sentence.

11. **look**   Action verb:

_____

_____

Linking verb:

_____

_____

12. **stay**   Action verb:

_____

_____

Linking verb:

_____

_____

Name _____ Date _____

Levels of Specificity and Irregular Verbs

Focus

When writers want to describe something the best they can, they try not to use a general word, but a word that is more specific and paints a certain picture for the reader.

We were impressed with the entertainer who loudly announced the next act—the animals.

We were impressed with the ringmaster who loudly announced the next act—the lions.

You know that the rule for forming the past tense of most verbs is to add -ed. **Irregular verbs** do not follow this rule.

- For example, *run* and *ran* are different by only one letter, and *go* and *went* are completely different words.

Practice A

Each general word below is followed by a more specific word used in "Jason and the Golden Fleece." On the line, write one more specific word for the general word.

1. chair → throne   chair →   _____

2. said → whispered   said →   _____

3. clothes → robes   clothes →   _____

4. monster → dragon   monster →   _____

5. entrance → gate   entrance →   _____

Practice B **Write the past tense of the following verbs.**

6. begin _____

7. choose _____

8. fly _____

9. sing _____

10. teach _____

Apply **Rewrite the sentences, replacing the underlined words with more specific words that mean the same thing. You will be surprised how much more interesting the sentences will be.**

11. I decided to read that <u>book</u> because it was about <u>animals</u>.

_____

_____

12. To get to the <u>building</u>, drive about five miles west on that <u>road</u>.

_____

_____

13. We watched a <u>performance</u> at the theater, then went home in a <u>vehicle</u>.

_____

_____

14. A <u>person</u> yelled at us when we swam out too far in the <u>water</u>.

_____

_____

Name _____ Date _____

Selection Vocabulary

Focus

assassins (ə • sas' • ins) *n*. plural of **assassin:** a person who murders a public figure, such as a government leader (page 614)

challenged (chal' • ənjd) *v*. past tense of **challenge:** call to take part in a contest (page 614)

worthy (wûr' • thē) *adj*. having enough value; deserving (page 614)

throb (throb) *n*. a heavy, fast beat or sensation (page 615)

hideous (hid' • ē • əs) *adj*. extremely ugly; horrible (page 616)

strait (strāt) *n*. a narrow channel between two larger bodies of water (page 617)

destiny (des' • tə • nē) *n*. what happens to a person, especially when it seems to be determined in advance; fortune (page 618)

glistening (glis' • ən • ing) *adj*. shining with reflected light (page 620)

pity (pit' • ē) *n*. a feeling of sorrow and sympathy for the troubles of another (page 620)

gaping (gā' • ping) *adj*. wide open (page 620)

Practice

Write the vocabulary word that best matches the underlined word or phrase in the sentences below.

1. The wet grass was <u>shining with reflected light</u> soon after the sun rose.   _____

2. I was <u>called to take part in</u> a basketball game.   _____

3. The liner sailed through the <u>narrow channel connecting two large bodies of water</u>.   _____

4. Elena had <u>sorrow and sympathy</u> for animals at the shelter.   _____

5. I felt a <u>heavy, fast beat</u> in my thumb after hitting it with the hammer.

_____

6. The agents caught the <u>people who murder a public figure</u> after their plans were discovered.

_____

7. The <u>extremely ugly</u> painting still hangs in my childhood doctor's office.

_____

8. To Jenny, the landing area on the aircraft carrier seemed <u>wide open</u>.

_____

9. At the carnival, the automated, fortune-teller game attempted to tell me <u>what happens to a person, especially when it seems to be determined in advance</u>.

_____

10. Andrea's speech was <u>having enough value of</u> the praise it received.

_____

Apply   Match each word on the left to its definition.

11. hideous

12. glistening

13. destiny

14. gaping

15. strait

a. a narrow channel between two larger bodies of water

b. wide open

c. very ugly; horrible

d. shining with reflected light

e. a feeling of sorrow and sympathy for the troubles of another

f. what happens to a person, especially when it seems to be determined in advance

Formulating Questions and Problems

A good question or problem to investigate:

_____

_____

_____

_____

_____

Why this is an interesting question or problem:

_____

_____

_____

_____

_____

Some other things I wonder about this question or problem:

_____

_____

_____

_____

_____

Formulating Questions and Problems (continued)

My investigation group's question or problem:

_____

_____

_____

_____

_____

What our investigation will contribute to the rest of the class:

_____

_____

_____

_____

_____

Some other things I wonder about this question or problem:

_____

_____

_____

_____

_____

Name _____ Date _____

Writing an Invitation

Audience: Who will read your invitation?

_____

Purpose: What is your reason for sending out invitations?

_____

Invitations provide brief, specific information about what the event is or why it is being held, when it will take place (including the date and time), where it will take place (including the address and sometimes directions) and who is giving the party. Use the organizer below to plan your invitation.

What: _____

Who: _____

When: _____

Where: _____

Given By: _____

Directions: _____

_____

_____

_____

_____

_____

Now, use a separate piece of paper to create a map to accompany your directions.

Revising   Use this checklist to revise your invitation.

☐ Have you included the details your audience needs to know?

☐ Is your language clear and concise?

☐ Does your invitation provide information about the reason for the event, the time, and the location?

☐ Did you provide clear cardinal and ordinal directions so your recipients can locate the event?

Editing/Proofreading   Use this checklist to make corrections.

☐ Is your invitation formatted correctly?

☐ Did you check all capitalization, spelling, and punctuation?

☐ Have you double-checked your directions and made sure you properly spelled the names of streets and landmarks?

Publishing   Use this checklist to publish your personal letter.

☐ Use spacing and design to enhance the appearance of your invitation.

☐ Neatly rewrite or type your invitation.

Name _____ **Date** _____

Spelling

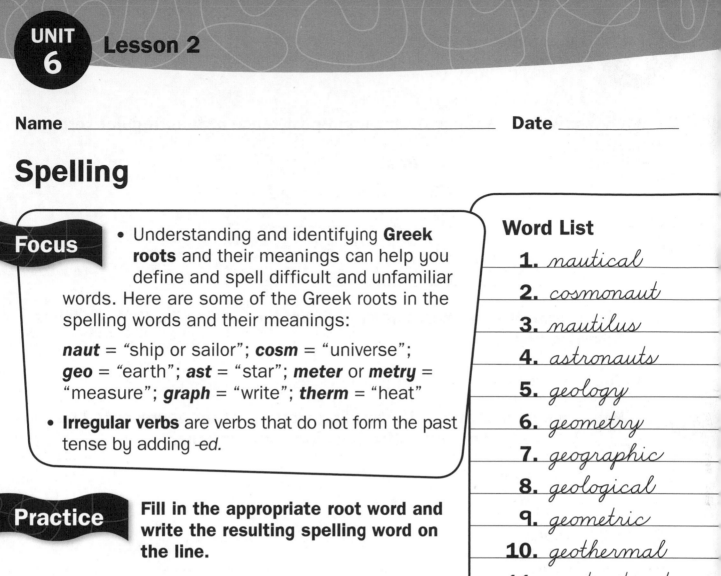

Focus

- Understanding and identifying **Greek roots** and their meanings can help you define and spell difficult and unfamiliar words. Here are some of the Greek roots in the spelling words and their meanings:

  naut = "ship or sailor"; **cosm** = "universe"; **geo** = "earth"; **ast** = "star"; **meter** or **metry** = "measure"; **graph** = "write"; **therm** = "heat"

- **Irregular verbs** are verbs that do not form the past tense by adding -ed.

Word List

1. nautical
2. cosmonaut
3. nautilus
4. astronauts
5. geology
6. geometry
7. geographic
8. geological
9. geometric
10. geothermal
11. understand
12. understood
13. teach
14. taught
15. forgive
16. forgave
17. forgiven
18. break
19. broke
20. broken

Practice   Fill in the appropriate root word and write the resulting spelling word on the line.

1. _____metry   _____

2. _____ilus   _____

3. _____metric   _____

4. geo_____ic   _____

5. _____logical   _____

6. _____nauts   _____

7. geo_____al   _____

8. _____logy   _____

9. _____nauts   _____

10. _____ical   _____

On the lines, write the present tense and past tense of the irregular verbs.

Present	Past
11. _____	12. _____
13. _____	14. _____
15. _____	16. _____
18. _____	19. _____

On the lines, write the two past participles from the spelling list that are forms of the following verbs.

19. break _____   **20.** forgive _____

Apply   On the lines, write the spelling words that are represented by the following root and suffix meaning combinations.

21. universe + sailor   _____

22. earth + logy   _____

23. earth + measurement + ic   _____

24. star + sailors   _____

25. earth + heat + al   _____

Select the correctly spelled word in parentheses that completes the sentence, and write it on the line.

26. A (nautilus, nawtilus) is a kind of sea creature.   _____

27. A valley is a (gealogical, geological) feature.   _____

28. My sister's favorite subject is (geometry, geomitry) _____

Name _____ Date _____

Compound Sentences and Plurals

Focus

A **compound sentence** consists of two or more simple sentences, which are also called independent clauses. The sentences should be connected by a comma and a conjunction, such as *and, or,* or *but,* or a semicolon.

The **plurals** of many words are formed by adding -s or -es.

- For words that end in a consonant and *y,* change the *y* to *i* and add -es.

    cherry, cherries   colony, colonies

- For some words that end in *f* or *fe,* change the *f* or *fe* to *v* and add -es.

    wife, wives   calf, calves

- For words that end in a consonant and *o,* you add either -s or -es.
    piano, pianos   echo, echoes

- For some words, the plural form is a different word.
    woman, women   tooth, teeth

- For some words, the singular and plural forms are the same.
    moose, moose   series, series

Practice A   **Combine each pair of sentences below into a single compound sentence.**

1. Dave wants to see a movie. I want to go skateboarding.

_____

_____

2. Shane met Donetta at the library. They studied together.

_____

_____

3. We can make dinner. We can order a pizza.

_____

_____

4. Krista trimmed the bushes. Krista raked the leaves.

_____

_____

5. The bus travels down this street. The street is closed for repairs.

_____

_____

Practice B Write the correct plural form of each singular noun listed below.

6. leaf _____

7. traveler _____

8. deer _____

9. city _____

10. person _____

Apply Place a check mark next to each sentence that is a compound sentence and an *X* next to each simple sentence. Then add the missing commas to the compound sentences.

11. _____ My friend and I built a model airplane and we displayed it at school.

12. _____ Our teacher was impressed with our finished product.

13. _____ Mr. Jefferson had flown the same kind of plane in the Air Force and he told us about his experiences.

14. _____ Paul always knew he would become a teacher or a pilot for an airline.

15. _____ He loves sharing his knowledge with others.

Name _____ Date _____

Irregular Plurals and Base Word Families

Focus

The plurals of many words are formed by adding *-s* or *-es*. **Irregular plurals** do not follow this rule.

- For some words, the plural form is a different word.
  man, men foot, feet

- For some words, the singular and plural forms are the same.
  trout, trout deer, deer

A **base word** is a word that can stand alone when all prefixes, suffixes, and inflected endings are removed. Identifying and understanding base words can help you definedifficult and unfamiliar words.

Practice A

For each singular word below, write its plural form on the line.

1. species _____

2. series _____

3. sheep _____

4. person _____

5. tooth _____

6. mouse _____

7. moose _____

8. woman _____

9. goose _____

10. foot _____

Practice B

Identify the common base word in the words below.

11. historical, historian, prehistoric _____

12. understanding, misunderstanding, understandable _____

13. acceptable, acceptance, accepted _____

14. agreement, disagree, agreeable _____

15. uncover, coverage, discover _____

Apply Read the following sentences. If the sentence contains a correct plural form, place a check mark on the line. If the plural form is incorrect, rewrite the sentence using the correct form. Use a dictionary if you need help.

16. _____ We love to watch the salmons swim in the stream.

_____

_____

17. _____ Several of the mans on the field ran to help the dog.

_____

_____

18. _____ We caught eight fish last time we went to that particular lake.

_____

_____

19. _____ Many of the pioneers used oxes to pull their wagons west.

_____

_____

20. _____ Both childs love to study dinosaurs.

_____

_____

Name _____ Date _____

Selection Vocabulary

Focus

sport (sport) *n.* amusement; fun (page 630)

descended (di • send' • əd) *v.* past tense of **descend:** to come down (page 630)

quest (kwest) *n.* a search or pursuit (page 631)

beaded (bēd' • əd) *adj.* covered with drops (page 631)

task (task) *n.* a piece of work to be done (page 632)

lumbered (lum' • bərd) *v.* past tense of **lumber:** to move about in a clumsy, noisy way (page 633)

exhausted (ig • zost' • əd) *adj.* weak or tired (page 634)

loyalty (loi' • əl • tē) *n.* strong and lasting affection and support; allegiance (page 635)

spring (spring) *adj.* from a place where underground water comes out of the earth (page 636)

fitter (fit' • ər) *adj.* healthier; in better physical shape (page 637)

Practice   Write the vocabulary word next to the group of words that have a similar meaning.

1. faithfulness; trustworthiness _____

2. chore; job _____

3. journey; search _____

4. wet with dew; covered in droplets _____

5. well; fountain _____

6. fell; plummeted _____

7. plodded; stumbled _____

8. healthier; more robust _____

9. recreation; amusement _____

10. emptied; depleted _____

Apply

Write the selection vocabulary word that best answers each question below.

11. If Reggie exercises for half an hour each day, what will he become?

_____

12. Which word describes snow that has fallen to the ground?

_____

13. Which word describes prospectors searching for gold?

_____

14. What does the outside of a glass of ice water become on a hot day?

_____

15. Hot water bubbling out of the ground is an example of what?

_____

16. Which word describes how a cow might have walked over uneven ground?

_____

Name _____ **Date** _____

Making Conjectures

Our question or problem:

_____

_____

_____

_____

_____

Conjecture (my first theory or explanation):

_____

_____

_____

_____

_____

_____

_____

_____

_____

As you collect information, your conjecture will change. Return to this page to record your new theories or explanations about your question or problem.

Establishing Investigation Needs

My group's question or problem:

_____

_____

_____

Knowledge Needs—Information I need to find or figure out in order to investigate the question or problem:

A._____

B. _____

C. _____

D. _____

E. _____

Source	Useful?	How?
Encyclopedias		
Books		
Magazines		
Newspapers		
Videotapes, filmstrips, and audio clips		
Television		
Interviews, observations		
Museums		
Other:		

Name _____ Date _____

Play Sketch, Week 1

Think | **Audience: Who** will read your play?

_____

Purpose: What is your reason for writing a play?

_____

Prewriting | Although the format for a play looks different from other writing, the plot still has the same structure as other forms of literature. Use the following graphic organizer to plan your play.

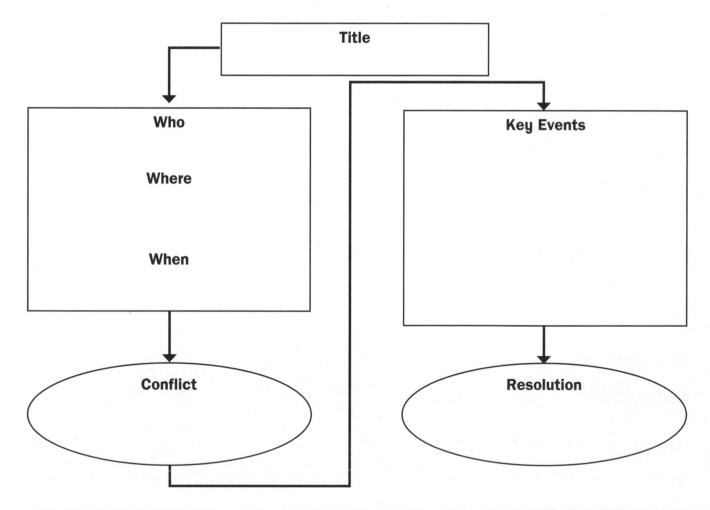

Drafting Use the lines below to create character sketches with your group for each of the main characters in your play. You may describe the way your characters look, feel, think, and act. You do not have to write in complete sentences. Use your sketches to help you as you draft your play.

Character #1: _____

Description: _____

_____

_____

Character #2: _____

Description: _____

_____

_____

Character #3: _____

Description: _____

_____

_____

Character #4: _____

Description: _____

_____

_____

Name _____ Date _____

Spelling

Focus

- A **base word family** is a family of words that share a base word. A base word can take many different forms when different prefixes, suffixes, and roots are added.

- The suffix **-ness** means "the state or quality of" or "capable or worthy of."

Word List

1. happiness
2. tiredness
3. timeliness
4. wickedness
5. coarseness
6. willingness
7. stiffness
8. sluggishness
9. laziness
10. selfishness
11. colony
12. colonial
13. colonist
14. colonization
15. company
16. companion
17. accompany
18. carried
19. carriage
20. carrier

Practice Add the suffix **-ness** to the following base words.

1. sluggish _____
2. willing _____
3. happy _____
4. wicked _____
5. selfish _____
6. stiff _____
7. timely _____
8. coarse _____
9. lazy _____
10. tired _____

For each word in the family, select the correct form of the base word to form the whole spelling word.

Base word: colony

11. _____zation _____
12. _____ist _____
13. _____ial _____

Base word: company

14. _____on   _____

15. ac_____   _____

Base word: carry

16. _____er   _____

17. _____ed   _____

18. _____age   _____

Apply   **On the line, write the spelling word that is related to each of the following words.**

19. sluggishly   _____

20. lazy   _____

21. time   _____

22. unhappy   _____

23. timeless   _____

In the following sentences, correct each underlined word and write it on the line. If the word is already correct, write *correct*.

24. The <u>kolony</u> in the New World grew slowly at first.   _____

25. My dog is a good <u>cumpanion</u>.   _____

26. Will we ever see the <u>colunization</u> of the moon?   _____

27. My father works for a large <u>company</u>.   _____

28. We <u>caried</u> our books to the library.   _____

Name _____ Date _____

Prepositions, Prepositional Phrases, and Apostrophes

Focus

- A **prepositional phrase** is a group of words that begins with a preposition and ends with the object of the preposition.

- A **preposition** shows the relationship between the main word in the phrase and another word in the sentence.
  He visited the house **near** the river.

Apostrophes are used to show possession.

- For most singular nouns, add *'s.*
  cat's ears, boss's necktie

- For plural nouns that end with s, add an apostrophe.
  flowers' petals, troops' uniforms

- For proper nouns that end in s, always add *'s.*
  the Harris's backyard, Chris's haircut

A contraction is formed by combining two words and omitting one or more letters. The **apostrophe** replaces the missing letters.
  do not, don't   we will, we'll   you have, you've

Practice A Underline the prepositional phrase(s) in each sentence.

1. Yao always took the same path to school.

2. Darren enjoyed visiting the animal shelter near the school.

3. Hannah enjoyed playing with her puppy until it was time for work.

4. After the game, Nitesh raced home to watch the news.

5. After his exercise routine, Gary always made sure to drink plenty of water.

Practice B **Insert apostrophes where they are needed in the following sentences.**

6. Im on my way to the Harriss annual barbecue.

7. This year theyre going to borrow the Cohens croquet set for the day.

8. In the past, theyve used our next-door neighbors volleyball net, but they had moved away recently.

9. Were bringing our familys folding chairs like weve done for every cookout.

10. Ill call you later tonight, and well discuss the days events.

Apply **Create a prepositional phrase, and write it on the line using the preposition in parentheses. Use the phrase in an original sentence.**

11. (under) _____

_____

12. (from) _____

_____

13. (beside) _____

_____

14. (against) _____

_____

15. (above) _____

_____

Name _____ Date _____

Possessives and the Prefix *pre-*

Focus

- Most **possessives** are formed by adding 's.
- For plural nouns that already end in s, just add an apostrophe.
- The prefix *pre-* means "before."

- Jess's house, a dog's collar
- the cars' horns, zebras' stripes
- preschool = before school

Practice A Change each singular possessive below into a plural possessive.

Singular	Plural	
1. messenger's drum	_____	drums
2. boy's bow and arrow	_____	bows and arrows
3. woman's stick	_____	sticks
4. tiger's neck	_____	necks
5. princess's eyes	_____	eyes
6. contest's winner	_____	winners
7. child's honesty	_____	honesty
8. wife's veil	_____	veils
9. necklace's stones	_____	stones
10. brave's gift	_____	gifts

Practice B

Add the prefix *pre-* to the following words, and then use each new word in a sentence.

11. planned _____

_____

_____

12. heat _____

_____

_____

13. treat _____

_____

_____

14. approval _____

_____

_____

15. washed _____

_____

_____

Apply

On a separate sheet of paper, use five of the plural possessives from the previous section in original sentences. In each sentences include one word with the prefix *pre-*.

Name _____ Date _____

Selection Vocabulary

Focus

Paraguay (par' • ə • gwā') *n.* a country in central South America (page 646)

murals (myo͞or' • əls) *n.* plural of **mural:** a picture that is painted on a wall. A mural usually covers most of a wall (page 646)

irritably (ir' • i • tə • blē) *adv.* in an angry or impatient way (page 647)

pleading (plē' • ding) *v.* making a sincere request; begging (page 647)

burdened (bûr' • dend) *adj.* weighed down with a heavy load (page 648)

noble (nō' • bəl) *adj.* having greatness of inner nature (page 652)

scowls (skoulz) *v.* frowns in an angry way (page 655)

rare (râr) *adj.* not often found (page 659)

intricate (in' • tri • kit) *adj.* involved or complicated, complex (page 660)

murmur (mûr' • mûr) *v.* to make or say with a low, soft sound (page 659)

Practice Choose the word that matches each definition below, and write it on the line.

1. _____ complicated; complex

2. _____ weighed down

3. _____ begging

4. _____ having inner greatness

5. _____ speak softly

6. _____ wall paintings

7. _____ impatiently

8. _____ South American country

9. _____ not often found

10. _____ frowns

Apply **Fill in each blank with the selection vocabulary word that best completes the sentence.**

11. Isabel was _____ with her coach to be put into the game.

12. After years of searching, the biologist found a _____ species of butterfly.

13. Some of our downtown buildings have colorful _____ painted on them.

14. Ideally, only _____ people would take part in politics.

15. My sister _____ every time I beat her at checkers.

Name _____   Date _____

Play Sketch

Think   **Audience: For whom** will you perform your play?

_____

Purpose: What do you want your performance to accomplish?

_____

Revising   Use the graphic organizer below to make sure your play has a beginning, a middle, and an ending.

Beginning: _____

_____

_____

_____

_____

Middle: _____

_____

_____

_____

_____

Ending: _____

_____

_____

_____

_____

Revising
Use this checklist to revise your play.

☐ Do the opening lines grab your audience's attention?

☐ Are your characters believable and well-rounded?

☐ Is your dialogue natural and realistic and appropriate for each character?

☐ Is the dialogue written at a level your audience will understand and enjoy?

☐ Does your dialogue and stage directions clearly describe the setting and show what happens?

Editing/Proofreading
Use this checklist to correct mistakes.

☐ Have you used the standard formatting for a play including dialogue and stage directions?

☐ Have you spelled the names of people and places consistently and capitalized proper nouns?

☐ Do your subjects and verbs agree?

☐ Have you checked that all dependent clauses are joined to an independent clause by a comma?

Publishing
Use this checklist to publish your play.

☐ Choose students to act out the roles in your play, and practice your performance.

☐ Perform your play for the class.

Name _____   Date _____

Spelling

Focus

- The prefix **pre-** means "before." It can be added to a word that begins with a consonant or vowel.
- **Multiple-meaning words** are words with more than one meaning but the same word origins.

Word List

1. prearrange
2. precaution
3. premature
4. preoccupied
5. prehistoric
6. prejudge
7. preload
8. preorder
9. precooked
10. predetermine
11. flounder
12. disposal
13. refrain
14. positive
15. manual
16. residency
17. general
18. resort
19. flourish
20. ground

Practice

On the line, write the spelling word that results when the prefix **pre-** is added to the word parts.

1. cooked   _____
2. judge   _____
3. caution   _____
4. load   _____
5. determine   _____
6. occupied   _____
7. mature   _____
8. order   _____
9. arrange   _____
10. historic   _____

On the line, write the spelling word that corresponds with the following pairs of definitions.

11. "to move or struggle" and "a kind of fish"   _____

12. "certain" and "greater than zero"   _____

13. "to grow strongly or thrive" and "to wave about boldly" _____

14. "earth or land" and "did grind" _____

15. "common or affecting everyone" and "a military officer" _____

16. use for "help" or "place for recreation" _____

17. "to hold oneself back" or "a phrase or verse in a song _____

18. "throwing away" or "the act of settling something" _____

19. "relating to or done by hands" or "instruction book" _____

20. "place one lives" or "training for a doctor" _____

Apply Match the appropriate spelling word to the phrase that best describes it.

21. worried _____

22. determine beforehand _____

23. load in advance _____

24. arrange beforehand _____

25. order in advance _____

Use context clues to determine the meaning of the underlined word and write it on the line. Use the definitions given on the previous page.

26. Do you know the <u>refrain</u> of that song?

_____

27. I like <u>flounder</u> better than trout.

_____

28. The plants will <u>flourish</u> with all this sunlight.

_____

Name _____ Date _____

Complex Sentences, Independent and Dependent Clauses

Focus
- A **complex sentence** contains an independent clause and one or more dependent clauses.

- An **independent clause** stands alone as a sentence.
- A **dependent clause** has a subject and a verb, but it cannot stand alone as a sentence.
- **Dependent clauses** modify words in sentences. They are used as either adjectives or adverbs.

- I found the book in the fiction section.
- I found the book **that Julie needed for school** in the fiction section.
- *That Julie needed for school* modifies the noun *book*, so it is being used as an adjective.

Practice A Label each sentence with *C* if it is a complex sentence or *X* if it is not a complex sentence.

1. _____ After Aziza finishes working on the computer, she logs out before turning off the power.

2. _____ The lights dimmed as the movie started, and everyone in the theater became silent.

3. _____ Maya's uncle, who visits a couple of times a year, always brings news about friends and relatives who still live in Dallas.

4. _____ The sheriff told the posse to head out while the sun still shone, and then he walked back inside the building.

5. _____ After Paul finished writing the novel, he got his book published.

Practice B — Underline the independent clause, and circle the dependent clause in each sentence.

6. After Jim's mom dropped us off, we headed to English class.

7. As the bus was pulling away, Jeremy ran out of his house to the bus stop.

8. Since the Shamrocks won the softball game, the entire town had a big celebration.

9. The dog always ran away after dinner, because he knew he was getting a bath.

10. Matt always got up early during the summer, because sometimes his grandfather would let him ride the tractor.

Apply — On a separate sheet of paper, combine each set of clauses below to create a complex sentence. Be sure to use one or more of the conjunctions, relative pronouns, and subordinating conjunctions from the box.

when	and	that	whenever
unless	than	because	so
after			

11. it's cold enough; my friend Donyell ice skates

12. Angelo studied at the library yesterday; it was much quieter

13. a special visitor was coming for dinner; I helped clean the house

14. Krista finds the map; she won't know the way to the reunion

15. they had sprayed with water; the fire fighters left; smoke continued to rise from the building

Name _____ **Date** _____

Homophones and Word Relationships

Focus

Homophones are words that sound the same but have different spellings and meanings.

The following word pair is an example of a homophone: *would* and *wood*.

Identifying and understanding **word relationships** can give you clues about the meanings of difficult and unfamiliar words.

Practice A   The underlined word in each sentence is half of a homophone pair. Write the other half on the line followed by its definition.

1. "Sometimes <u>our</u> guests bring little gifts."

_____ Definition: _____

2. "She was used to getting her <u>way</u>."

_____ Definition: _____

3. "She cut a <u>piece</u>, wrapped it in a cloth napkin, and brought it upstairs . . ."

_____ Definition: _____

4. "Helen <u>ate</u> the cake very quickly . . ."

_____ Definition: _____

5. "The two weeks in the garden house <u>passed</u> quickly . . ."

_____ Definition: _____

Practice B — Identify how each word group is related, and write it on the line.

6. treadmill, jump rope, weights, medicine ball

_____

7. green beans, corn, spinach, carrots

_____

8. quatrain, lyric, free verse

_____

9. expository text, historical fiction, biography, realistic fiction

_____

10. drums, xylophone, tuba, saxophone

_____

Apply — Circle the homophone that correctly completes each sentence below.

11. It has been nearly a (weak, week) since the last snowstorm.

12. Will (their, there) be cake and ice cream at the party?

13. The tables at the park are made of (steal, steel).

14. Take a (peek, peak) at this note I am giving to Sydney.

15. Shawn looked (threw, through) the newspaper for coupons.

Name _____ Date _____

Selection Vocabulary

Focus

soiled (soild) *v.* past tense of **soil:** to make or become dirty (page 674)

lunged (lunjd) *v.* past tense of **lunge:** to move forward suddenly (page 675)

distract (dis • trakt') *v.* to draw one's attention away from what one is doing or thinking (page 675)

amusing (ə • mū' • zing) *adj.* entertaining (page 675)

imitating (i' • mi • tāt' • ing) *v.* acting just as another person does; copying (page 675)

sulking (sulk' • ing) *v.* acting angry and silent (page 676)

aromas (ə • rō' • məs) *n.* plural of **aroma:** a pleasant or agreeable smell (page 677)

remark (ri • märk') *n.* a short statement or comment (page 677)

disturbed (dis • tûrbd') *adj.* upset or confused (page 678)

insistently (in • sis' • tənt • lē) *adv.* in a strong or firm manner (page 678)

Practice **Write the word that best completes each sentence.**

1. Casey was _____ Mrs. Ito when she suddenly walked into the room.

2. The fair was filled with the _____ of cotton candy and fried food.

3. Antoine misheard the principal's _____ and thought he was in trouble.

4. I was _____ by an accident I saw on the freeway.

5. The mud on the bottom of my shoes _____ the rug.

6. Everyone found the playful puppies to be quite _____.

7. I was thrown back into my seat when the taxi _____ forward.

8. I tried to _____ my parents, while my sister placed their birthday presents.

9. After his team had lost the game, Jim would not stop _____.

10. Because it was almost time for the bank to close, Andy _____ requested the location of the bank.

Apply   Place a check mark next to the correct example for each selection vocabulary word.

1. Which is an example of something **amusing?**

_____ a clown juggling at a circus   _____ a car waiting at a stoplight

2. Which is an example of someone making a **remark?**

_____ a teacher praising your work   _____ a friend laughing at a joke

3. Which is an example of **imitating?**

_____ copying the way an actor speaks   _____ wearing a suit and tie

4. Which is an example of being **disturbed?**

_____ dropping your notebook   _____ realizing you are lost

5. Which is an example of something that is **soiled?**

_____ T-shirt with pizza sauce on it   _____ house that needs paint

Name _____ Date _____

Making Inferences

Focus Writers often do not include every detail about a character or an event in the story. Readers must use clues from the text to make inferences in order to complete the picture. **Making inferences** means using the writer's clues, and your own prior knowledge and experiences, to gain a better understanding of the character or event.

Practice Find two sentences in the selection from which you can infer something about Annie's character. Write the page numbers and sentences below. Then write a phrase telling the inference you made about Annie's character from the sentence.

1. Page: _____

Sentence: _____

_____

_____

What the reader can infer about Annie from this sentence:

_____

2. Page: _____

Sentence: _____

_____

_____

What the reader can infer about Annie from this sentence:

_____

 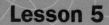

Apply Use your prior knowledge to make inferences based on each of the following sentences.

Example:

You look out the window and see people wearing heavy coats, hats, and gloves.

Inference: *It is cold outside.*

3. You hear pots and pans banging in the kitchen, and you start to smell something good.

Inference: _____

4. Fred didn't feel good yesterday, and he is not at school today.

Inference: _____

5. Every time Susan goes to Ted's house, his cat jumps into her lap and purrs.

Inference: _____

6. The dog gobbles up the beef treats you give him but spits out the chicken ones.

Inference: _____

Name _____ Date _____

Writing a Realistic Story

Think   **Audience: Who** will read your realistic story?

_____

Purpose: What do you want your readers to think about your story?

_____

Prewriting   One of the most basic rules that good writers follow is "show; don't tell." Using the lines below write a sentence describing part of the character's personality or an emotion. Then, write one or two sentences showing the character demonstrating this characteristic.

Character 1

Telling: _____

Showing: _____

_____

_____

Character 2

Telling: _____

Showing: _____

_____

_____

Revising
Use this checklist to begin revising your draft.

- ☐ Have you developed your characters enough? Are they believable?
- ☐ Does your story have a believable conflict, rising action, climax, and resolution?
- ☐ Did you write realistic dialogue for each character?
- ☐ Are the settings in your story vivid and believable?
- ☐ Did you delete irrelevant or repetitive ideas and consolidate similar ideas?

Editing/Proofreading
Use this checklist to begin editing your draft.

- ☐ Are the names you have invented for people and places realistic?
- ☐ Have you spelled the names of people and places consistently throughout your story?
- ☐ Do the key events of your story happen in a logical order?
- ☐ Did you check for correct, consistent verb tense and correct any misused words?

Publishing
Use this checklist to prepare for your next draft.

- ☐ Neatly retype or rewrite your story and include any illustrations.
- ☐ Place your story in your Writing Portfolio so you can evaluate your growth.

Name _____ Date _____

Spelling

Focus

Understanding and identifying **Latin roots** and their meanings can help you define and spell difficult and unfamiliar words. Here are some of the Latin roots in the spelling words and their meanings:

anim = "life, spirit"; **spec** = "see"; **mob** = "move"; **rupt** = "break"

Word List

1. animate
2. animal
3. animation
4. inanimate
5. animosity
6. inspect
7. spectacle
8. spectator
9. speculate
10. expect
11. mobile
12. automobile
13. mobility
14. mobilize
15. immobile
16. rupture
17. erupt
18. bankrupt
19. abrupt
20. interrupt

Practice

Fill in the appropriate Latin root and write the spelling word.

1. in_____ate _____

2. _____tacle _____

3. auto_____ile _____

4. _____ure _____

5. inter_____ _____

6. _____ulate _____

7. in_____t _____

8. _____ilize _____

9. _____ation _____

10. bank_____ _____

11. e_____ _____

12. ex_____t _____

13. ab_____ _____

14. _____tator _____

15. _____ility _____

16. _____ile _____

17. _____ate _____

18. _____osity _____

19. im_____ile _____

20. _____al _____

Apply Decide which Latin root correctly completes the word in each sentence. Write the spelling word.

21. Please do not inter_____ when someone is speaking. _____

22. They were im_____ile with fear. _____

23. A rock is an in_____ate object. _____

24. We tried to _____ate the tired group. _____

25. We ex_____t to get a lot of rain this week. _____

26. There was a _____ure in his thigh muscle. _____

27. Do not make a _____tacle of yourself. _____

28. You can sense the _____osity between the cat and the dog. _____

29. Our auto_____ile is stopped at the light. _____

30. That volcano may e_____ at any minute. _____

If the underlined spelling word is misspelled, correct it. If the word is already correct, write *correct*.

31. My favorite <u>anamal</u> is a horse. _____

32. The troops began to <u>mobalize</u>. _____

33. The company finally went <u>bankruped</u>. _____

34. They <u>inspecked</u> all of the suitcases. _____

35. Is that an old <u>mobile</u> phone? _____

Name _____ Date _____

Misused Verbs, Pronouns, and Modifiers and Appositives

Focus

- An important part of writing well is being able to recognize misused words. By carefully rereading what you have written and listening closely to how each word is used, you can spot verbs, pronouns, and modifiers that have been used incorrectly.

- An **appositive** is a noun that modifies or renames another noun or pronoun.

  My school, **DuBois Elementary,** is a fun place to learn.

- An **appositive phrase** is an appositive and the words that modify it.

  Uncle Chris went to France, **a country in Europe,** to study art.

Practice A   Circle the verb that correctly completes each sentence below.

1. Yesterday my brother and I (road, rode) the bus downtown to the library.

2. It (was, were) the first time I ever traveled on the bus without my mom.

3. We (set, sat) near the front of the bus in the last available seats.

4. At the library, my brother (learned, taught) me how to search for a book using the computer.

5. We (look, looked) in three different sections before finally locating the book.

Practice B

Underline the appositive or appositive phrase in each sentence. If there is no appositive in the sentence, write an _X_ on the line.

6. _____ My youngest brother, T. J., collects baseball cards.

7. _____ Rollie, the oldest brother, was idolized by all the younger kids in the neighborhood.

8. _____ The baseball glove in the window was not for sale.

9. _____ My oldest sister, Francesca Leon, is a marine biologist.

10. _____ The spinner dolphin, a type of dolphin that rotates in the air, jumps high out of the water and spins up to 14 times before landing.

Apply

The sentences below contains numerous misused words. Read each sentence carefully, and then rewrite it correctly on the lines that follow.

11. Lonnie think its more fun to skateboard then it is to ride a bike.

_____

_____

_____

_____

12. When I rose my hand, the teacher says, "You can make one more comment, but than we need to move on."

_____

_____

_____

_____